A Halifax Boyhood

growing up on the city's outskirts in the 1940s and 50s

Malcolm MacLeod

Visuals selected by

William D. Naftel

My part in this book was small Bob, but my birthday wishes for you are huge.

Formac Publishing Company Limited

Halifax

To Heather, well-loved wife for life

Formac Publishing Company Limited recognizes the support of the Province of Nova Scotia through the Film and Creative Industries Nova Scotia. We are pleased to work in partnership with the agency to develop and promote our creative industries for the benefit of all Nova Scotians. We acknowledge the financial support of the Government of Canada through the Canada Book Fund for our publishing activities. We acknowledge the support of the Canada Council for the Arts for our publishing program.

FILM & CREATIVE INDUSTRIES NOVA SCOTIA

The Canada Council for the Arts | Le Conseil des Arts du Canada

Canada

Library and Archives Canada Cataloguing in Publication

MacLeod, Malcolm, author

A Halifax boyhood : growing up on the city's outskirts in the 1940s and 1950s / Malcolm MacLeod.

Issued in print and electronic formats.

ISBN 978-1-4595-0328-1 (pbk.).--ISBN 978-1-4595-0329-8 (epub)

1. MacLeod, Malcolm--Childhood and youth. 2. Halifax (N.S.)--History--20th century--Pictorial works. 3. Halifax (N.S.)--Biography. I. Title.

FC2346.26.M33 2014 971.6'22504092 C2014-903099-1 C2014-903100-9

Formac Publishing Company Limited
5502 Atlantic Street
Halifax, Nova Scotia, Canada
B3H 1G4
www.formac.ca

Printed and bound in Canada

FSC www.fsc.org MIX Paper from responsible sources FSC® C004071

Contents

CHAPTER 1 1941

Ice Cakes

Parts of the northwest arm of Halifax Harbour can freeze over in January and February during the worst weeks of winter. This happened more often back in the 1940s than during the recent era of global warming. When it froze, there still remained a strip of separately floating ice cakes along the water's edge, where tidal action kept the ice broken up. The whole situation was a perfect trap for the unwary, venturesome little boy. Indeed, it almost killed me.

I became a Haligonian at age four, when my family moved from Lunenburg. Not quite Haligonian actually, for the new home was on the other side of the Northwest Arm in Melville Cove, still unamalgamated. We settled into a small home right on the edge of that beckoning, treacherous salt water.

In that very picturesque neighbourhood, Melville Island was the leading landmark. It was formerly the sight of a prison, but its buildings were now empty. It was several years later that the Armdale Yacht Club took over the property. When I first saw it, the causeway road to Melville Island ran through a gateway in a high stone wall that had spikes and broken bottles set sharply in the top of it to discourage excursions by long-past generations of prisoners. Next to the island, moving south along the shore, was the prison commandant's residence. It was a two-storey brick structure turned derelict; it had no doors or windows, and I would not say that everyone had avoided performing some bodily functions inside that ruin. Facing the Arm, the front yard was as spacious as a softball field — in fact (much later), it was in that very ball field that I missed making my first outfield catches.

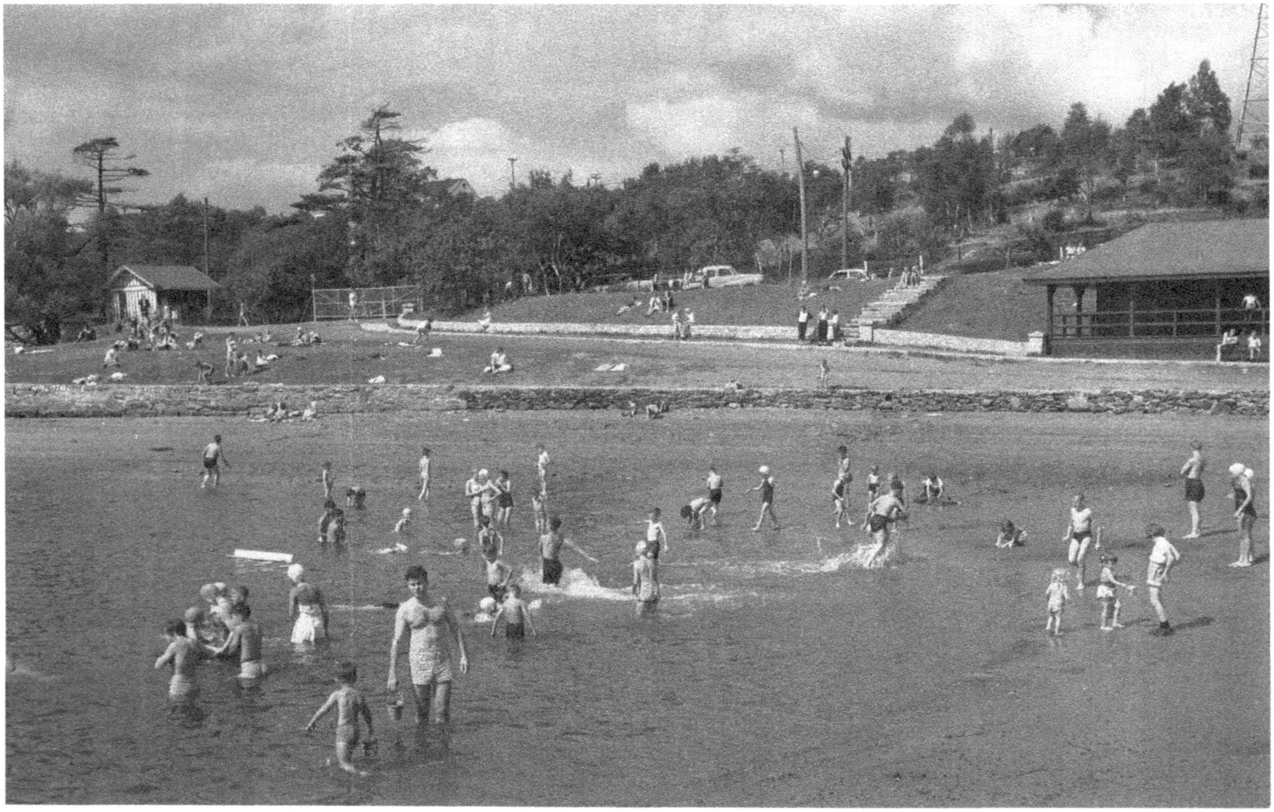

Horseshoe Island

Beyond the commandant's field was a residential area, which could be accessed via a lane that headed steeply down from Purcell's Cove Road. Ours was the second or third house, right along the shoreline: a small, brick, one-storey place. My parents always called it the "cottage," which makes me think that the fireplace I remember was likely the only means of heating. There was also a wood- or coal-fed stove in the kitchen.

For the next half-mile, south along the shore, there were more homes, the forest of Fleming Park, and then the commanding, photogenic, memorial tower at the cute little cove called "the Dingle." About the same distance on the other side of the Arm was Horseshoe Island, where generations of children learned to swim with chattering teeth. More or less right across from our place was the row of boat clubs that gave the Arm its sporty reputation: the Jubilee, which hardly counted since it was mostly for dancing, and the more athletic, monied leisure of the St. Mary's, Waegwoltic and Northwest Arm rowing clubs.

The area where we lived was right at the water's edge, and thus particularly dangerous, especially

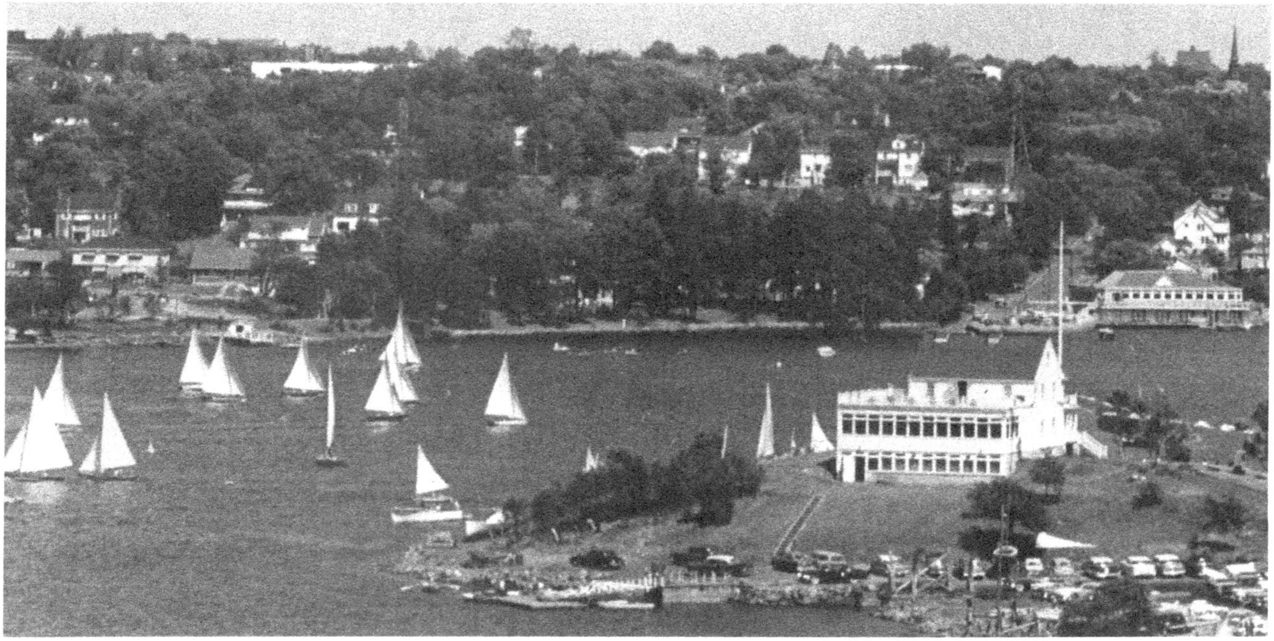

Melville Island, September 1963

for little children. Mother told a story about how, when we moved in, there was another boy even younger than I was living in the house behind us. One raw, overcast fall day, she saw him dejectedly wandering the lawn that sloped down to a low seawall at the edge of their property. When she looked out again, five minutes later, he was not there. Another half hour, and she saw a police car and ambulance. After that, the house in back was silent; blinds shrouded all the windows, and there was no little boy.

For older children and adults, the Arm eventually became a safe enough, usable playground: swimming in summer, skating in winter. Another sport, combining aspects of both activities, was jumping lightly from one ice cake to another to get to the solid part of the ice. It took athleticism and good balance, and an indifference to being suddenly immersed in freezing water. When I was about eight — we had moved to a different place, still right on the shoreline — I remember one of my little pals demonstrated that he did not yet have the knack. He jumped from shore to the edge of an ice cake and slipped into the water. He went right under, but fortunately, when he got to his feet, the water only reached his waist. Did he ever bellow! He was roaring when he came up, as he clambered out of the water, and as he ran home. Ever helpful, I grabbed a stick and snagged his cap that had been left floating and followed along with it. Perhaps I expected huge praise for this rescue; my friend's mother, however, seemed to ignore me as she quieted her boy and took him inside to get warm again.

Back to our first winter as Haligonians, when we

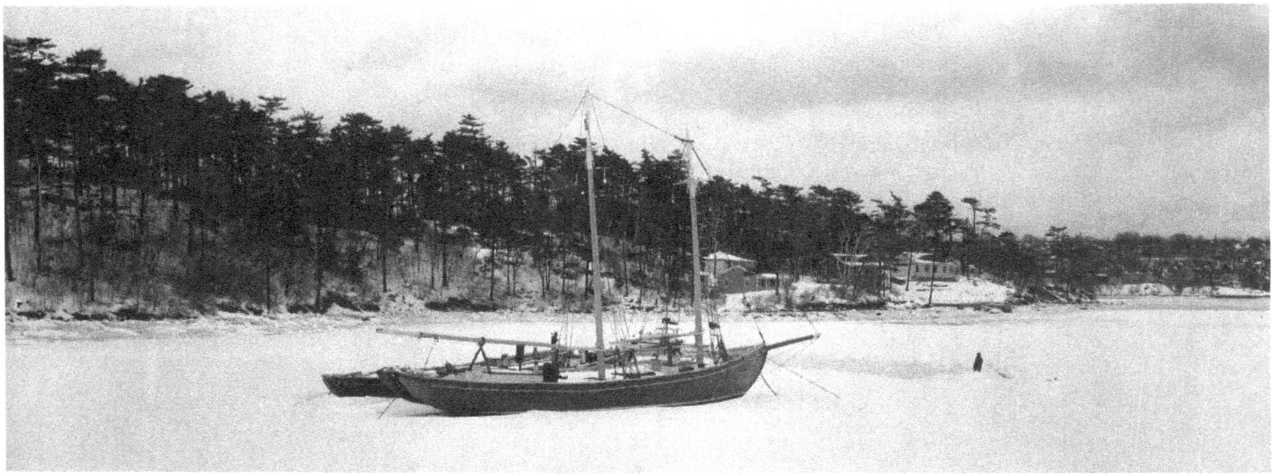

A frozen Northwest Arm

were still keeping an eye on that promising, death-dealing Northwest Arm. Around February, Mother dressed my sister Marlene and me, and put us outside. We were probably going to walk — on the roadway, not the ice — "down the Arm" to the corner of Quinpool and Chebucto roads, and a couple of blocks farther to go shopping at Simpson's big store.

Mother had to go back inside for something. She insisted afterwards that she told me to stay right where I was. When she was out of sight, I first moved a few inches away from that spot, then a few feet. No thunderbolt descended to reinforce the parental command.

A minute or two later, Marlene came skipping along and saw my wool cap with the red bunny ears lying on the ice near shore. She went to pick it up and, what a surprise, I still had it on my head! Bobbing between the ice cakes, I was buoyed by a lot of air trapped in my bulky winter clothing. She gave out a holler from sturdy six-year-old lungs, and teenaged boys playing hockey nearby came over and fished me out.

This story may not be true. I have heard about it numerous times, but I have no independent memory of the event. I do not recall the shocking plunge into freezing water, nor the spot where I was supposed to stand and wait, nor the cute woolen cap with red bunny ears. So this is a case similar to twenty-first-century government press releases about terrorist plots: Some parts of the story may have solid foundation in fact, parts may be incomplete or misleading, parts may be fabricated, and we have no way of knowing which are which.

Years later, Dad and one of my younger sisters also needed to be rescued from that same risky inlet. About my own pseudo-memory from the time I was four, all we can say for sure is that something apparently happened, and it made me the first in my family to join the lucky legion of folks living up and down that dangerous shoreline with bragging rights to claim, I survived the Northwest Arm!

CHAPTER 2 1941–59

Down the Arm

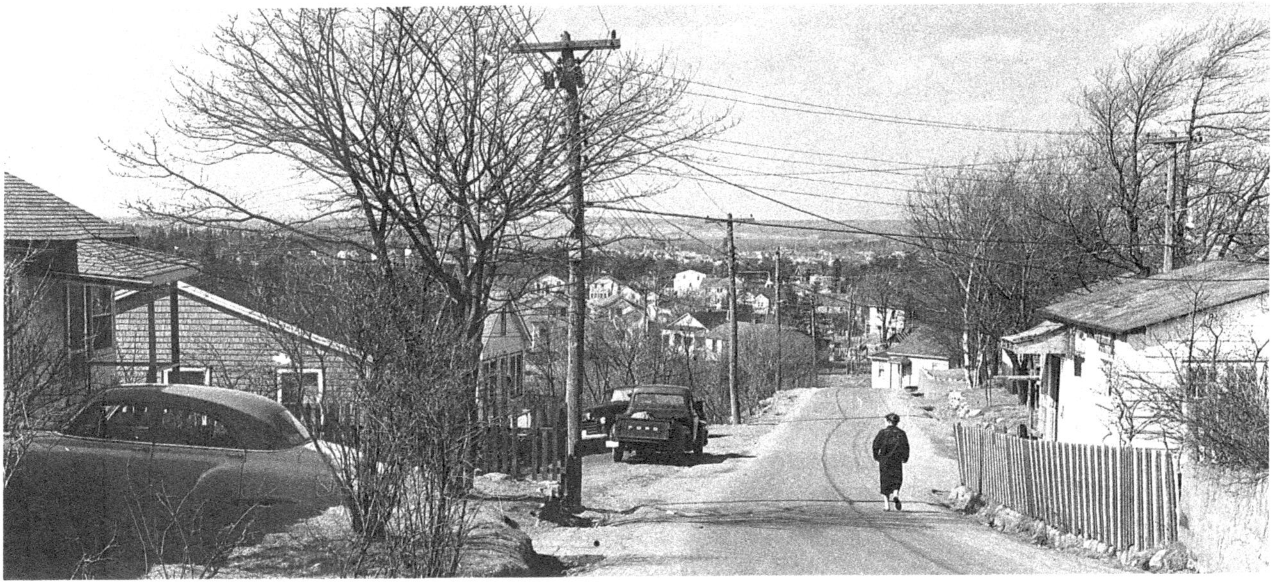

Kline Heights looking east on Withrod Drive, 1957

Our first home in the county suburbs was in Melville Cove; later we moved to Kline Heights. In both cases, the distance to the nearest part of the city of Halifax was about a half a mile. Since this memoir is dedicated to old Halifax, we can linger a little to recall the landmarks along the routes we took. Frequent repetition embedded them in memory for a lifetime. When I was young, I walked to that intersection of Herring Cove Road, Quinpool and three other streets literally thousands of times.

The earliest attraction that drew us to the Arm

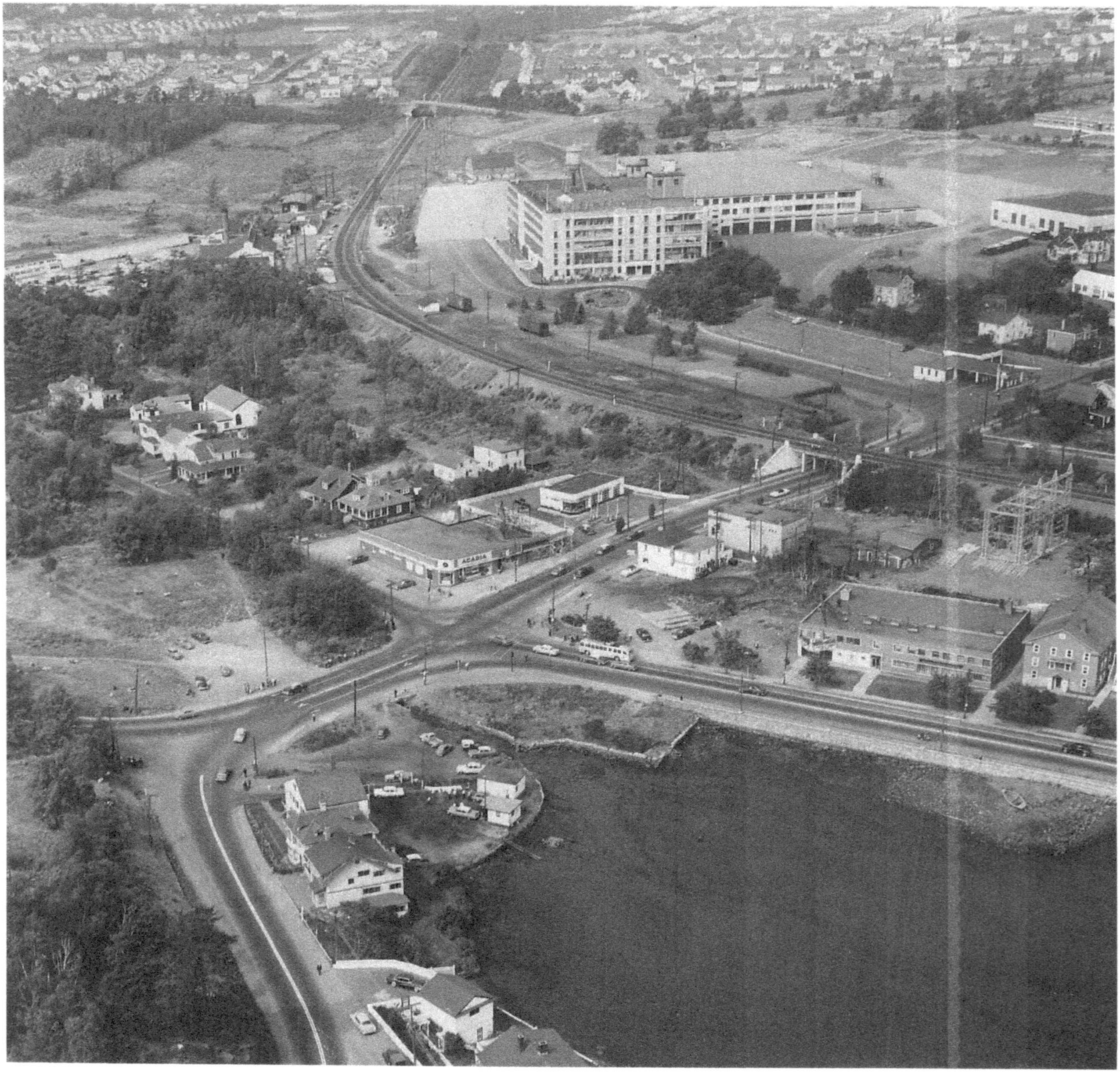

Armdale in 1957, prior to the construction of the Rotary. "The Nova Scotia Highways Department will spend $65,000 to improve the traffic conditions of the Armdale Rotary." (Herald, *September 1957)*

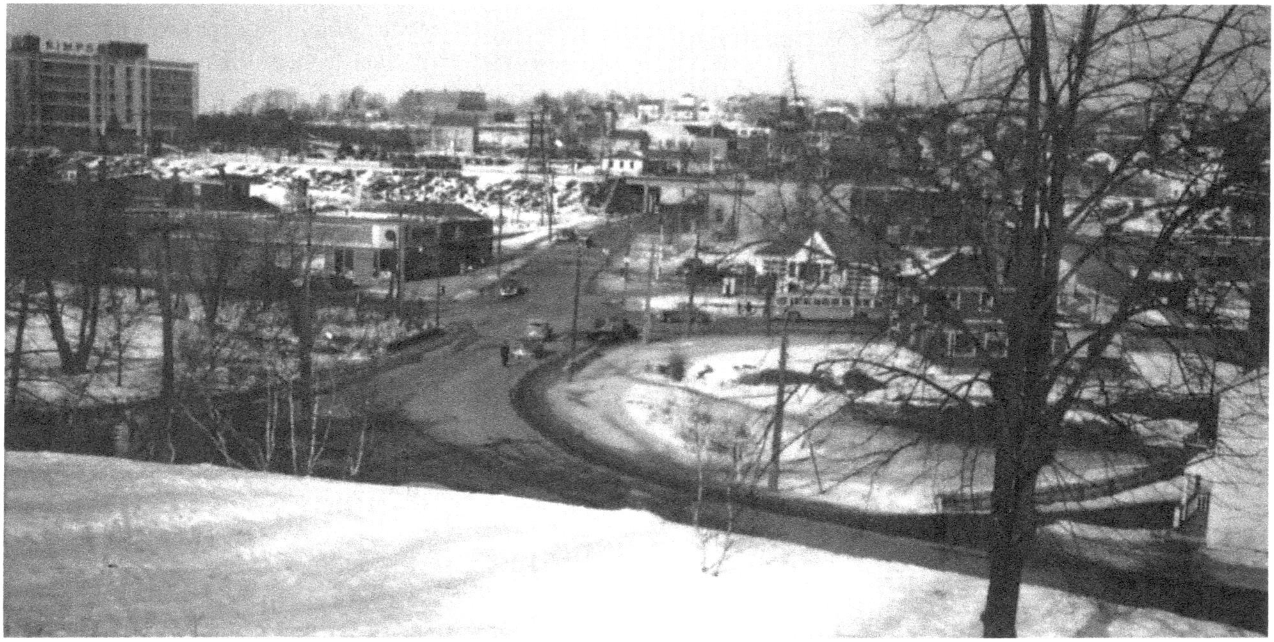

Pre-rotary intersection of Quinpool, Chebucto, Dutch Village and other roads

corner was Simpson's department store. It was just a couple of blocks up Chebucto Road, after passing under the rail overpass where the little Armdale rail station (last stop before downtown Halifax) was located. Other important destinations, also nearby, were

- the city transit stop at the foot of Chebucto Road. Initially tram cars and later trolley coaches paused there after turning a circle in front of Simpson's. The Number 5 went in town by way of Quinpool and Cogswell, turned right on Hollis Street and made another circle in front of the Nova Scotian Hotel to head back to Armdale.

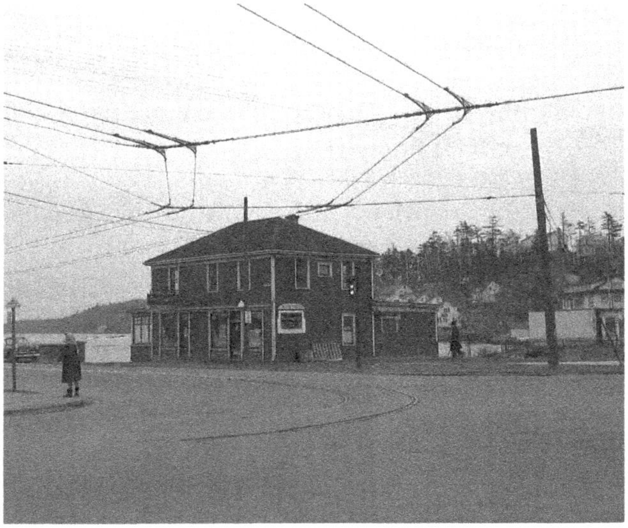

Bert's Tearoom, January 1959

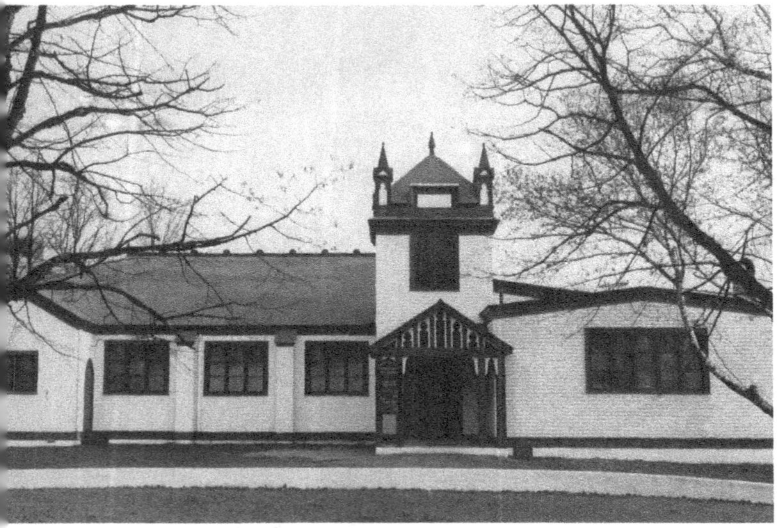

Above: Old Bethany United Church circa 1930
Opposite: Simpson's

- our church, Old Bethany United, a short distance along Dutch Village Road.

- a movie theatre.

- the post office, when there was a parcel to send or collect.

- the Armview Grill, where we liked to hang out during certain teenage years, until asked to leave for noisily taking up so much space while spending so little money.

- the grassy field between St. Margaret's Bay Road and Dutch Village Road, which accommodated impromptu softball games whenever a half dozen or more boys happened to be present.

The approved language for referring to that oft-repeated walk was "goin' down the Arm." This was verbal shorthand for "down to the Arm." Looking back now, I see that what we meant by "the Arm" was not perfectly precise, or consistent. As time passed, "the Arm" had four different meanings.

First of all, it meant the head of the Northwest Arm: the furthest spot inland reached by that picturesque narrow bay on the west side of Halifax Harbour. This usage goes back a long way; I wonder if the Mi'kmaq language has a phrase for it.

Secondly, there was the idea: going down to the Arm bridge. There used to be a little stream flanking the trail to St. Margaret's Bay. This rivulet required a bridge to pass under Herring Cove Road. I have seen sketches of the bridge from the 1800s. They show an arched structure — wooden, rustic, romantic. Later, engineers got busy and channelled the stream into secret pipes and culverts. The stream still comes down the slope and passes under Herring Cove Road, but does so completely out of sight. When I was young, oldtimers still sometimes said, "goin' down the Arm bridge." I picked up that language and have used it myself, but it was long before my time that a real and noticeable bridge actually stood there.

Thirdly, and when I first started making that walk, "goin' down the Arm" meant walking to the intersection of Quinpool and Chebucto roads. As the place closest to home where one could catch city public transit, that was a highly strategic spot. Then traffic engineers got busy again and redesigned the whole area into its fourth configuration — the life-risking lottery known as the Armdale Rotary or Roundabout.

From that time, "goin' down the Arm" has meant walking to the rotary to try and find a way

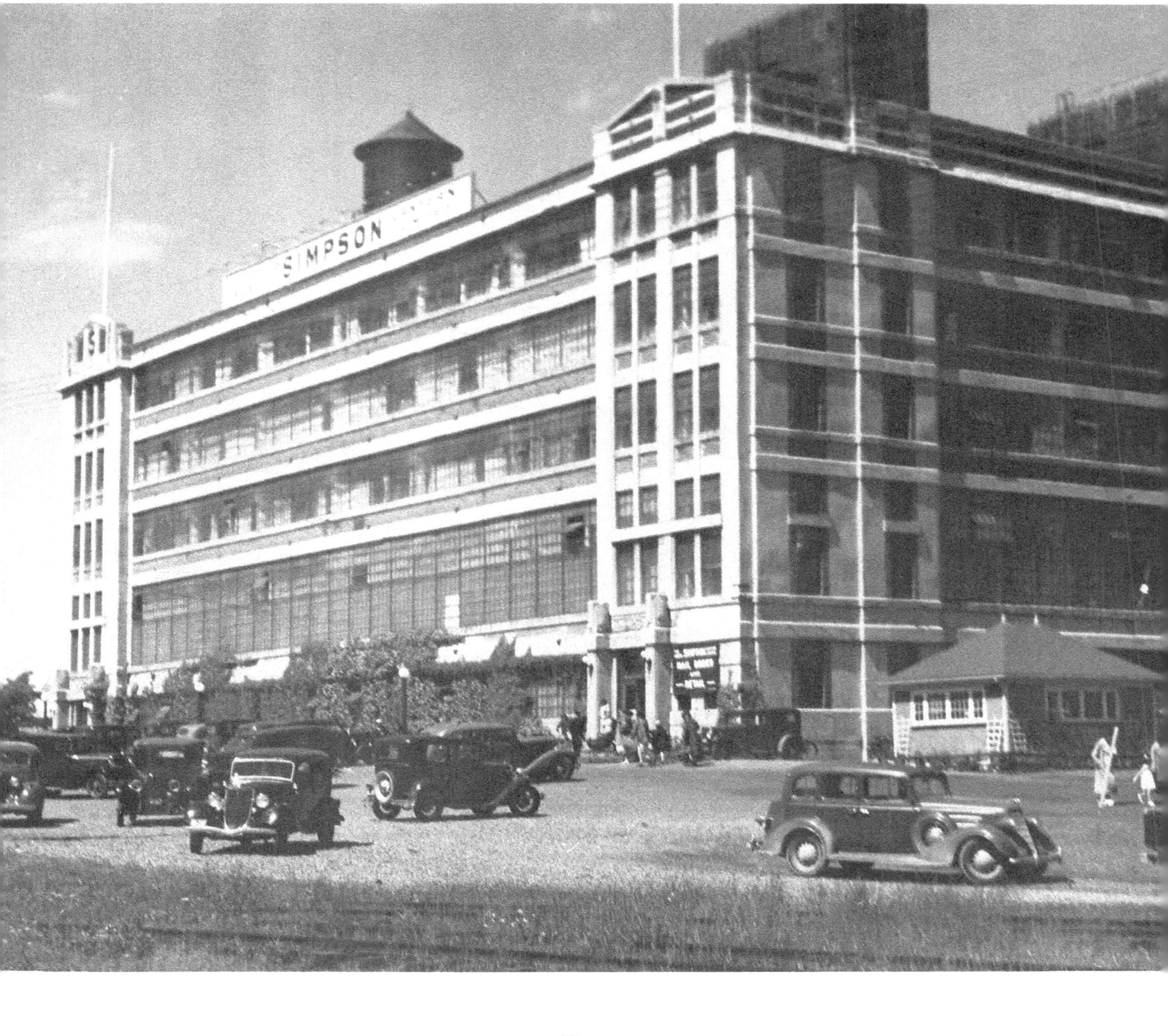
SIMPSON

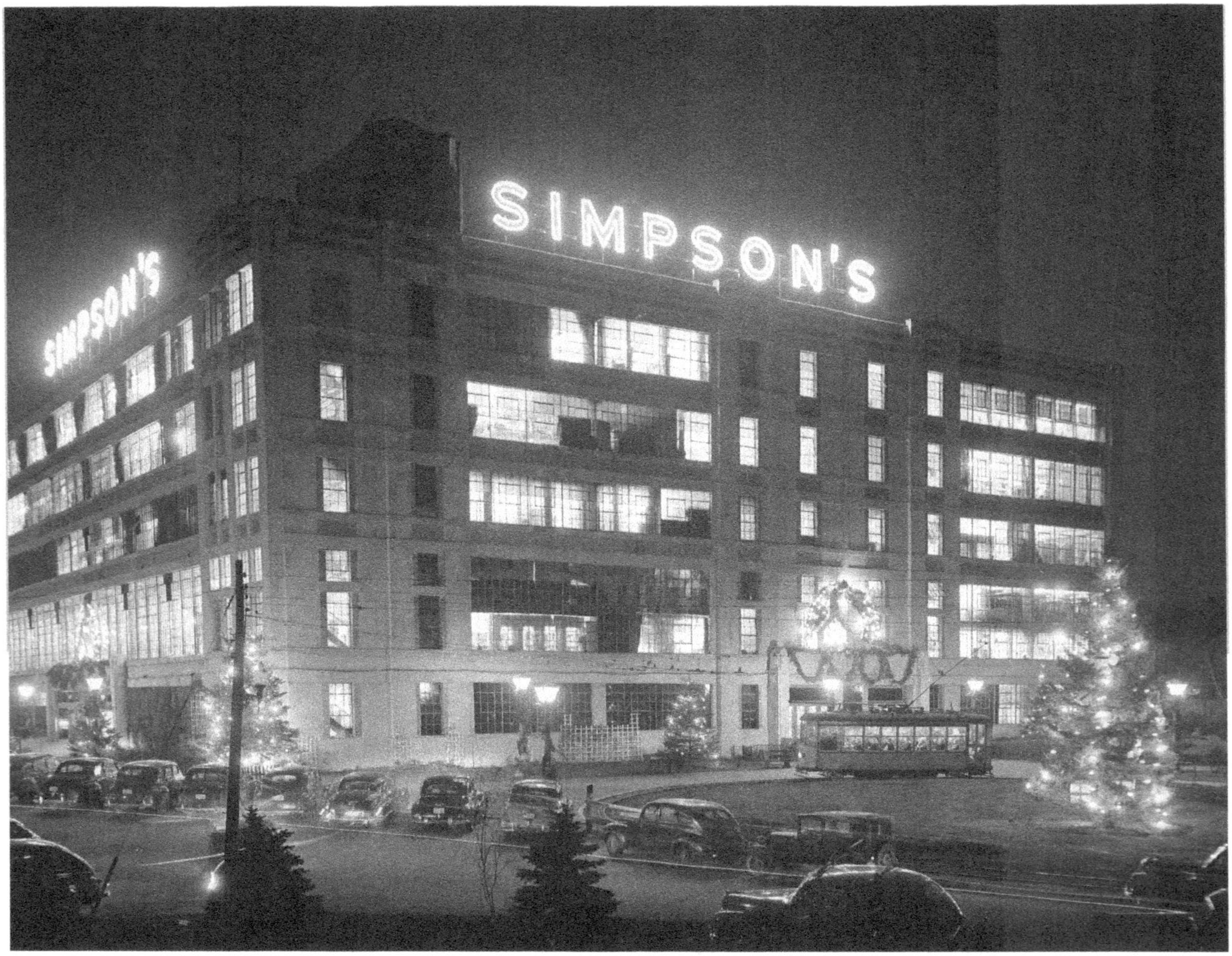

Simpson's at Christmas, 1948

across or around it. This fourth version requires more daring and athleticism than previous ones.

In my own experience, the earliest reason for "goin' down the Arm" was to accompany Mother shopping at Simpson's (the durable, big building set well back from Chebucto Road, which later housed Sears Bargain Centre). Stubby little legs found it a long walk from Melville Cove. It was well worth it, however, because of visits to the soda fountain and the fun of watching the elevator operator ply his difficult trade.

Manipulating his control lever, the elevator man always managed to stop a little above, or a little below, where the elevator was supposed to

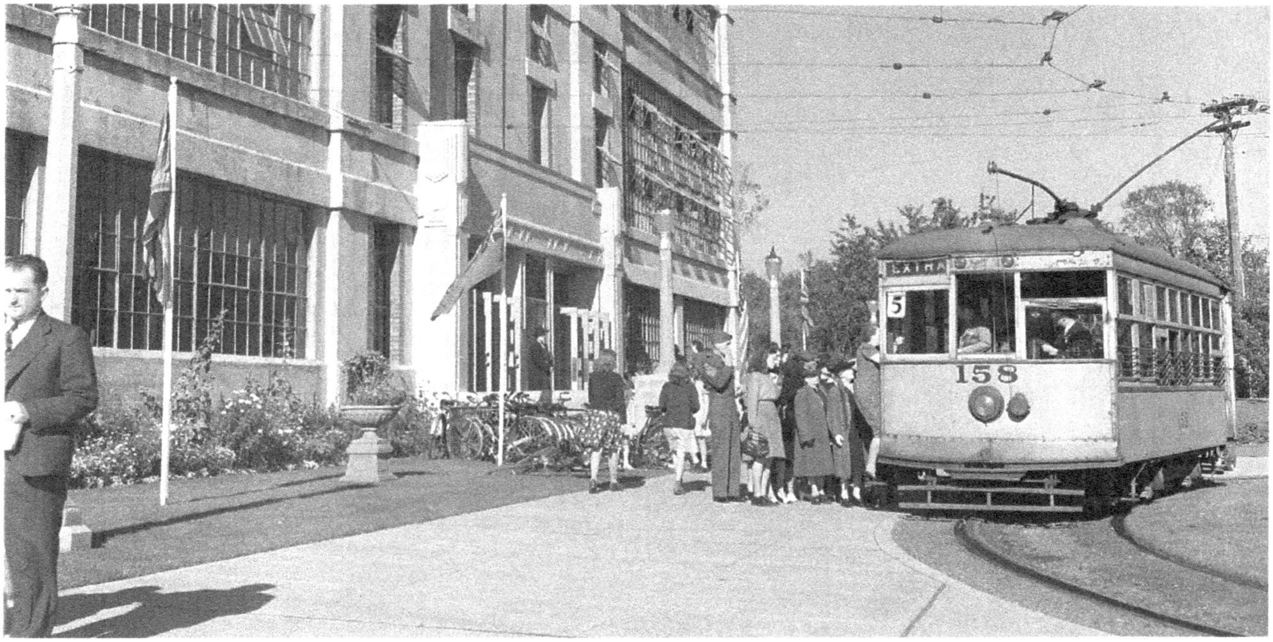

Number 5 tram car turning in front of Simpson's

be. It was fun to try to guess which it would be this time. At the soda fountain, I would have a milkshake. The shake itself was tasty, of course, but the best part was that the metal container in which the whirring machine beat it up was larger than the glass into which the waitress poured it. She put your milkshake on the counter in front of you, and right alongside it, the extra part. You finished your shake, then you reached over and poured your glass half full again. Getting an extra portion like this never happened with treats at home. I always thought of it as a shake and a half, beating the system.

While I was growing up, the same landmarks — with little change or development — punctuated the walk "down the Arm." We started the journey to the Arm from Melville Cove, walking along Purcell's Cove Road. The first landmark was the dilapidated old Melville Island Prison on a little island just offshore, reached by a causeway. The road curved inland, came up a slope and there, on the right, were the church, hall and school of St. John the Baptist Roman Catholic parish. Up a further slope was South Armdale School, across from a medium-sized grocery store called IPC (International Provisions, it was part of a chain) and tucked between two merging streams of traffic.

After we moved, the walk to the Arm from Kline Heights only provided one memorable landmark up to this spot: Bedley's. Bedley's, at the corner of Herring Cove Road and Withrod Drive, was a convenience store with basic groceries, hardware, toys, clothes, maybe books, certainly comics — an amazingly large and varied

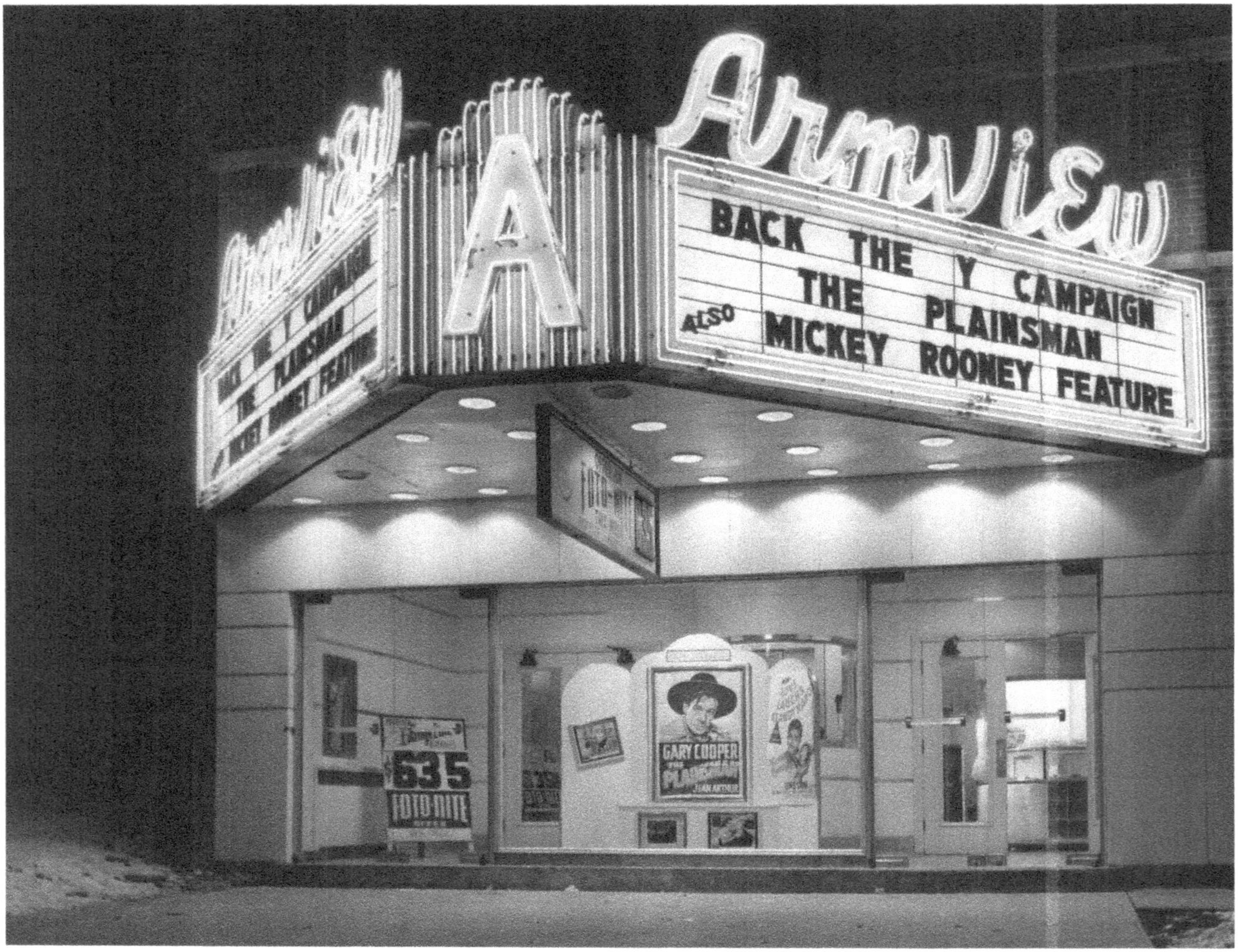

The theatre, originally called the Hyland, which faced the Quinpool Road entry to the Rotary

inventory squeezed into a very small space. Two of everything, the motto could have been: one to sell and one to gather dust. They also operated a French fries canteen during evening hours.

After Bedley's came a nice level stretch, as far as the IPC intersection where Purcell's Cove Road comes up to join Herring Cove Road. Chocolate lake was and is on the left. Over its spillway, facing traffic, lake overflow began a very rapid descent towards the Northwest Arm. Follow the road steeply downhill, take a turn to the left and you are at the head of salt water where the Arm bridge used to be.

CHAPTER 3 1943–46

Cunard School

Today, if you mention Cunard School, people are bound to ask, “Where’s that?” When you explain that it used to be in Jollimore, many long-time residents of Halifax will still say, “Where’s that?”

Jollimore is a very private, almost secret little place halfway along the west shore of the Northwest Arm, seaward from Melville Cove and the Dingle. People are hardly aware of it, even if they rush past to get to Purcell’s Cove. When there used to be a school in Jollimore, it too was located in a very private space, at the furthest southerly side of the village on a dead-end street. Very few people would take that route on their way somewhere else; there were no casual passersby.

The school had an ample playground that one reached first, if walking or driving in from the road. At the far end of the property was the school itself. It had just one storey facing the playground, but showed two storeys in back, as the land there sloped sharply downhill. There were two classrooms on each level, thus four teachers. There was no kindergarten. Eight grades were accommodated in the four classrooms, two grades per room and teacher. This cosy location was the first school I attended (from grades 1 to 4), and the only one from which I was ever expelled.

Cunard School was just over a mile from our home — about three times farther away than South Armdale School. Nevertheless, some quirk of school catchment boundaries made Cunard our designated school. My older sister and I both went there, but it was not easy at first.

Marlene’s difficulty was the bus. After her first day of school, she missed it. An older girl from the neighbourhood had promised to help her out, but forgot. There was a period of panic

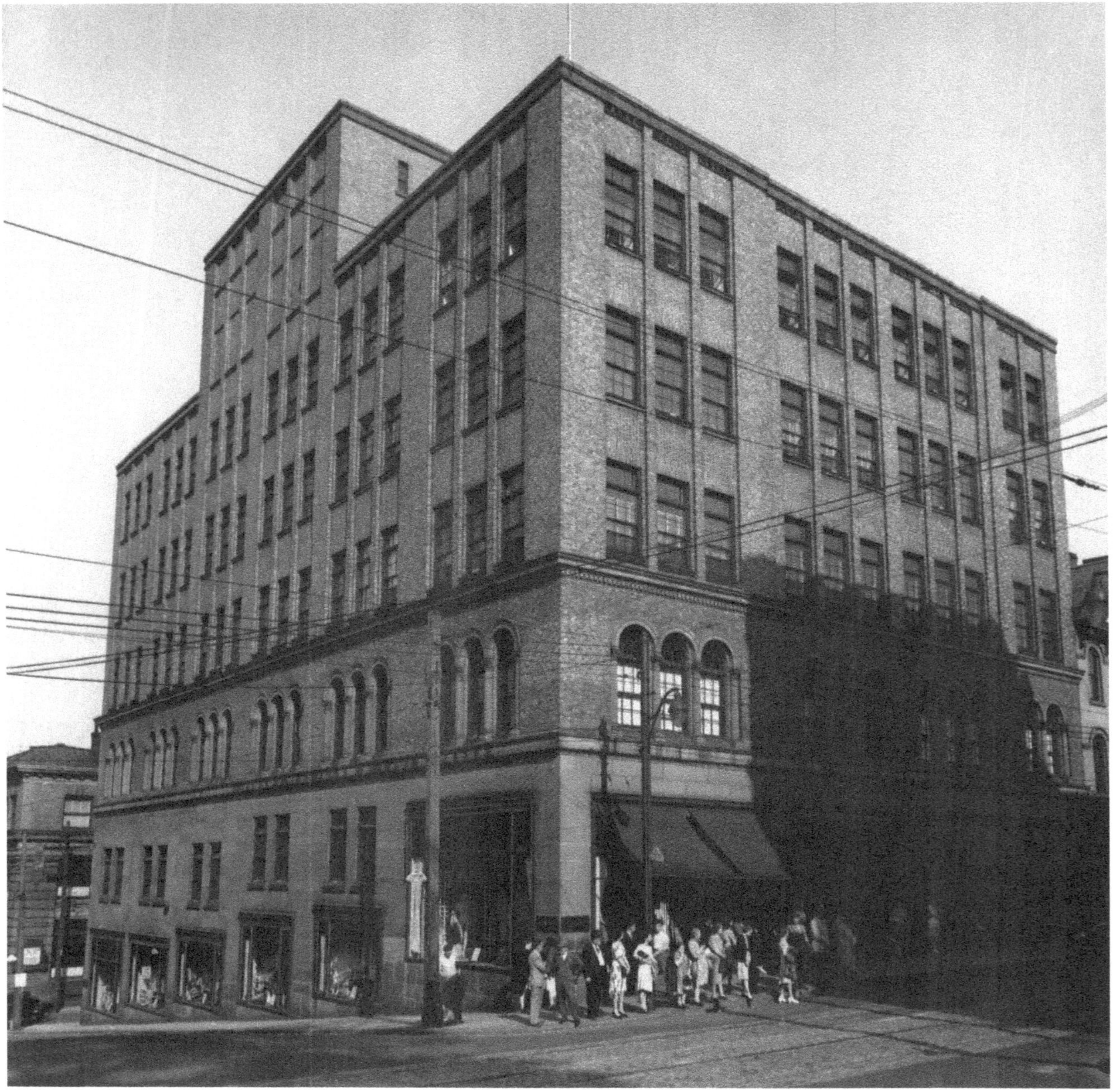

Eaton's store, Barrington Street (lending library)

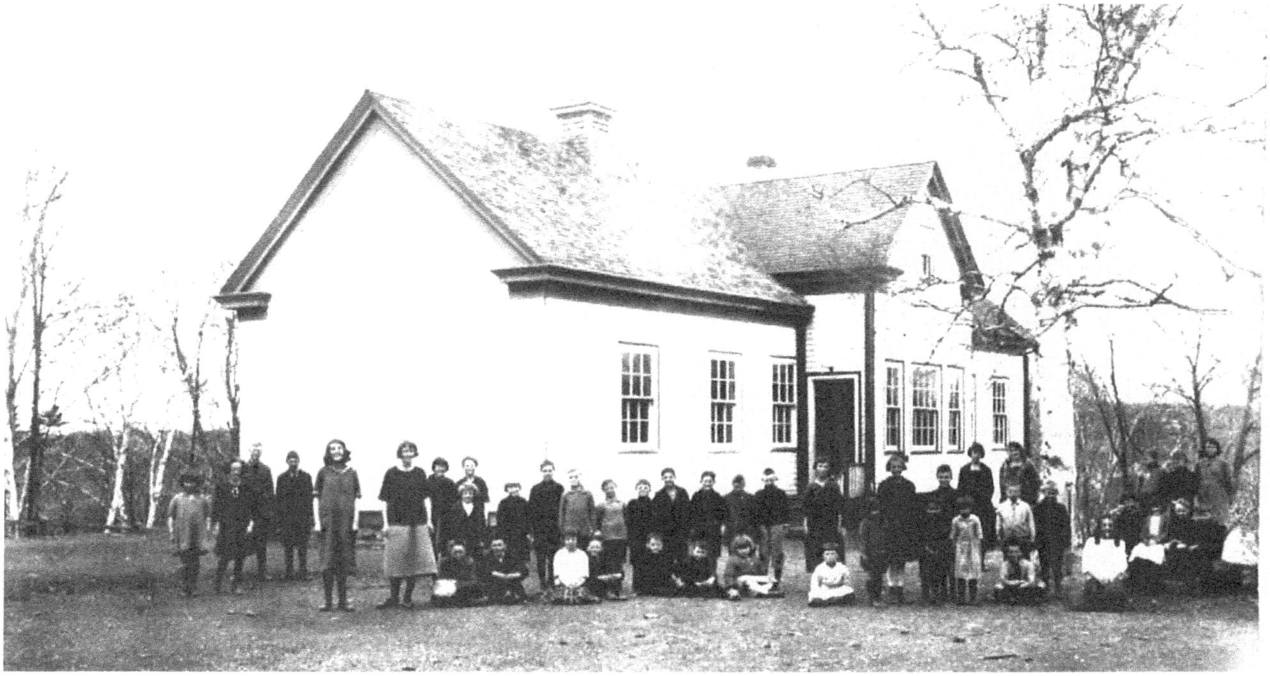

Old Cunard School, before the 1946 fire

before Marlene turned up safe. Mother then decided she was too young to go to school anyway, and kept her home. Interestingly, she did not tell Dad. A few weeks passed before he learned, from neighbourhood gossip, that Marlene was not in school. This revelation probably caused a scene in the family; I do not recall. Anyway, Dad then paid the small fee that permitted Marlene to attend South Armdale. It was within walking distance, and on the first day after New Year's, Dad went late to work to walk with her and make sure she was properly enrolled. Marlene returned to Cunard in Grade 3, when I was ready to start school so that she could make sure my initiation went smoother than hers had.

This precaution, however, did not work. I was rejected by Cunard School because of a personal deficiency. School eligibility rules were being rigidly applied, and in September, I was still five weeks shy of my sixth birthday. I was told to come back in January.

Nevertheless, I won the teacher's heart that first day, so they say. In her Grade 1 and 2 classroom, some of the pupils were practising handwritten capital letters, and I — tongue protruding from the side of my mouth with the effort, no doubt — was trying to keep up. One of the letters defeated my best attempts; I think it was either the H or the F. "I'm sorry, Miss Smith, I can't make that one," I said, and went on to cushion the blow: "And it's so pretty too."

I came back to Cunard after New Year's and worked to catch up with the other Grade 1 children.

Although I spent three and a half years of my primary school experience in this secluded corner of quiet Jollimore, I recall very few specifics about my time at Cunard. There are just two memories that stand out. One is the reading race. With the help of Uncle Mel, who read the daily newspaper's comic strips over the radio at suppertime — and no doubt with a lot of assistance from parents and teachers too — I quickly learned to read. Then I became voracious. When Mother showed me the lending library at Eaton's (Barrington Street), I realized that a lifetime might not be long enough to read all the interesting items that were available. The race was on.

Each of the four classrooms in Cunard School had a cabinet of books appropriate for that age group. Since I was among the more distant-dwelling children who stayed for lunch, I had plenty of time to read. The result was, after finishing the little items in our Grade 1 and 2 bookcase, I received special permission to keep going. By the time I left Cunard School at the end of Grade 4, I had completed reading what was available in Grade 3 and 4, and Grade 5 and 6, and was starting in on the offerings in the Grade 7 and 8 bookcase.

Another brief, vivid memory is of the principal on one particular occasion, a woman whose name I forget. She was usually quite dour and reserved, even stern. But here she is, one April morning when I was in Grade 3, girlishly dancing into our room in the middle of a lesson. "The war is over, the war is over," she singsonged, and danced out again. We all went home for the rest of the day to worry whether the *Bedford Magazine* — the radio said the building was on fire — was going to blow up.

After Grade 4, we moved to a new house in a different school district. I never saw Cunard School again, as it burned down shortly afterwards.

CHAPTER 4 1942–45

Learning to Swim

Despite our short season for it, around Halifax and Nova Scotia nearly everyone masters the mechanics of swimming. As a young child, I was somewhat unathletic, and this — accentuated by a lie my parents told me — resulted in my failure to learn to swim as easily or as early as most children manage to do.

When I was six, we moved to a new place. As it was still right on the shore of the Northwest Arm, my parents thought it a wise precaution to outfit my older sister and me with life preservers. Then, if we started floating away, we might at least be on top of the water. My life preserver slid on over my head like a sweater. It had thick pads in front and back, and tied around the waist. Mother and Dad explained it would hold my head above water. The mistake I made was believing them. They never mentioned that if someone plunged from a height, he would first go under — perhaps a long way under — before bobbing to the surface again.

Secure in my new preserver, I waded out to a pyramid-shaped boulder just offshore, near our backyard. Marlene was still in the house, looking for her bathing cap. Dad was so certain about this new preserver, he had not even stripped down to bathing trunks, ready for a rescue. Mother had the twins in their double perambulator ("pram"), ready to go for a stroll once dripping daughter and soaking son were safely back on land.

I jumped from about two feet above the surface into a five-foot depth of the Arm. I regret to remember, Americanized as I was, that I was shouting "Geronimo." The nationalist that would have insisted on "Ontario" or "Saskatchewan" had not yet emerged in me. I went under, of course, and took in a huge, distasteful swallow of evil salt water:

the North Atlantic, with a suggestion of outboard motor oil and other fumes, and a touch of sewage not entirely excluded. It was scant comfort that I did bob up again. Thrashing, crying and protesting, I made my way ashore and stormed into the house. I was finished with everything marine for some time.

CHAPTER 5 1945–46

The Dingle

Tranquil beauty showcased by respectful landscaping, the Dingle (officially, Sir Sanford Fleming Park) is the most special locale in all of Halifax. The park is on the west side of the Northwest Arm, a short distance seaward from the old prison (later, yacht club) on Melville Island. It is laid out in three concentric rings.

At the heart of Fleming Park is a work of nature: the half-circle cove with a sand-and-pebble beach that was the original Dingle. Arrayed around the beach are the works of humans: wharves and floats, a marina, roads, parking lots, canteen; and did I mention a hundred-foot-high stone tower with its entrance guarded by two bronze lions?

The manicured lawn, ribboned by walks and boasting a bandstand, slopes down to the seawall. The third, outer ring is a thick screen of wild forest, mostly spruce and pine that — except on the southern periphery, where the village of Jollimore abuts more closely — protects the sculpted heart of the park from the intrusion of residential neighbourhoods.

In my boyhood I was lucky — by the mere accident of where we happened to live and where we went to school — to become intimately familiar with the Dingle's layout and features. The children who lived in Melville Cove and attended Cunard School in Jollimore usually had bus transportation, but sometimes, either by choice or necessity, we walked. When we did, the shortest shortcut was right through the Dingle. I forget the first time this happened. It was probably after school one day, when the bus left without us.

I remember a group of three or four boys cutting right down to the Northwest Arm below the school and walking along the shore. We came to

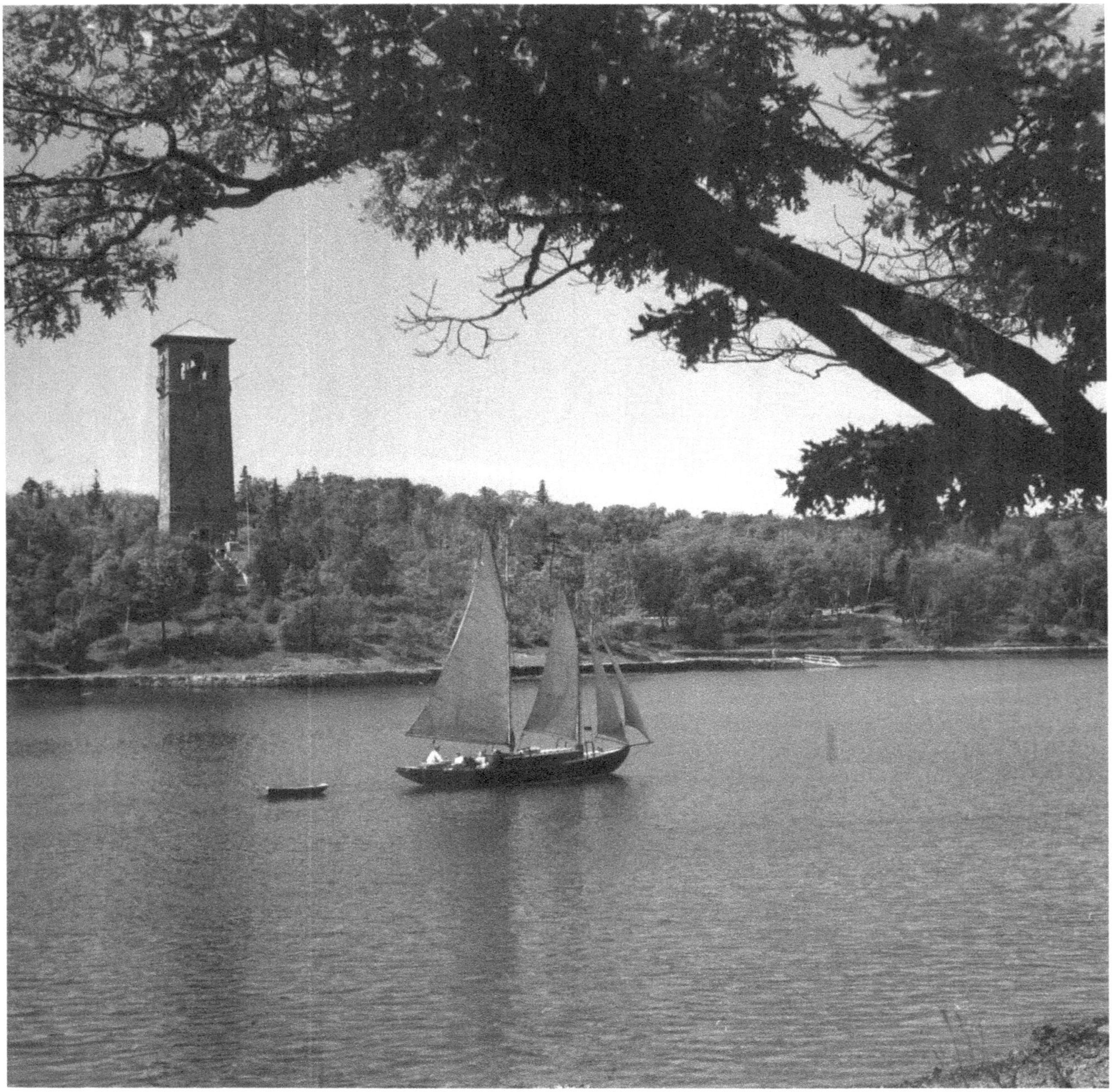

Dingle tower seen from the Halifax side

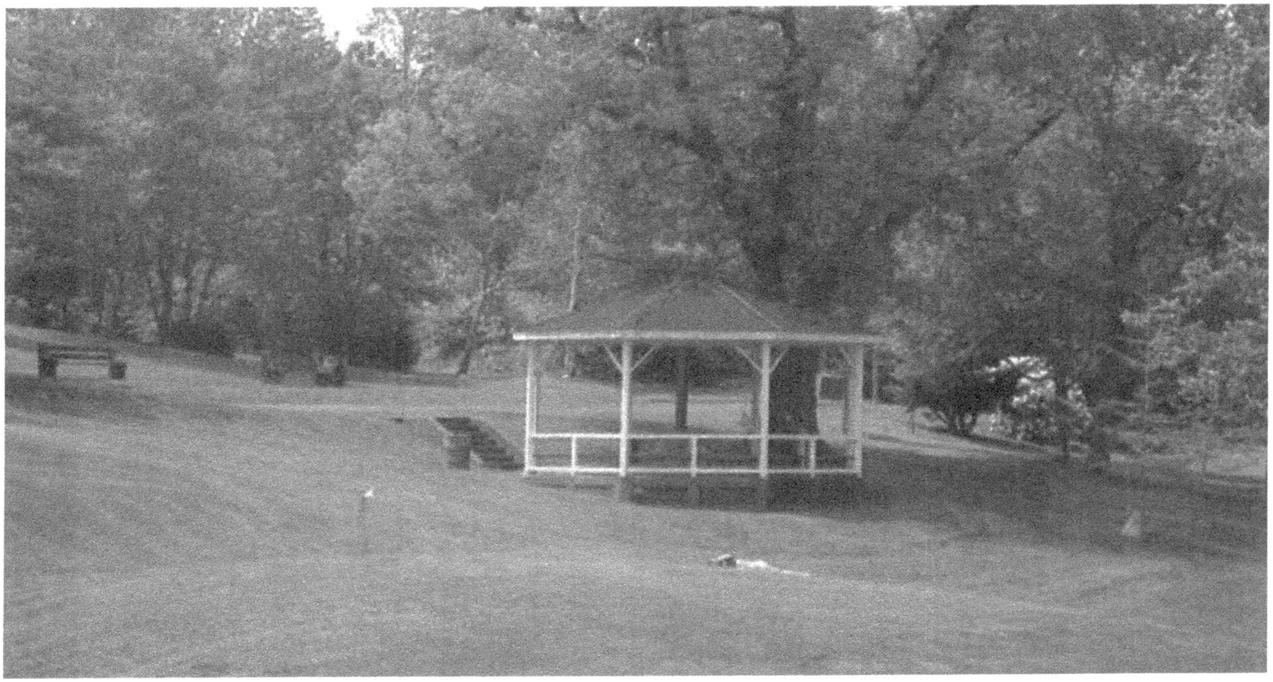

View of the bandstand

the marina, then to the stone tower erected forty years earlier to commemorate the oldest elected assembly in the second British empire. We tried the tower doors; they were locked. We shouted in through the narrow slit windows and echoed the echoes that came back. We climbed on the two ornamental, larger-than-life lions who were stationed alongside the entrance. I whispered something to my lion; he gave a low growl that nobody else heard. We tried the tower doors again.

We ran past the canteen and its parking lot, the circular beach and its little wavelets. Several young mothers were pushing their babies in carriages. We scampered across the lawn, balance-walked the low seawall and the railing around the bandstand. A couple of squirrels scolded us from overhead. Only the very occasional car passed as we walked along the curving paved road that went up an easy rise to the park gates.

Halfway up the road, on the left, a little brown brook bubbled and sloshed along. It slanted down a green hill; Coleridge (we were reading him in school) would have said "athwart." There was a path alongside the brook, which was the shortest route to our school. Soon, on the other side of the road, we came to the cottage (originally Sir Sanford's) occupied by the groundskeeper and his family. It must have been autumn, for there were apples hanging in the small, adjoining orchard. One of the boys picked one. Although innocent, I ran with the others when the lanky groundskeeper, Mr. Schmeisser, emerged bellowing from

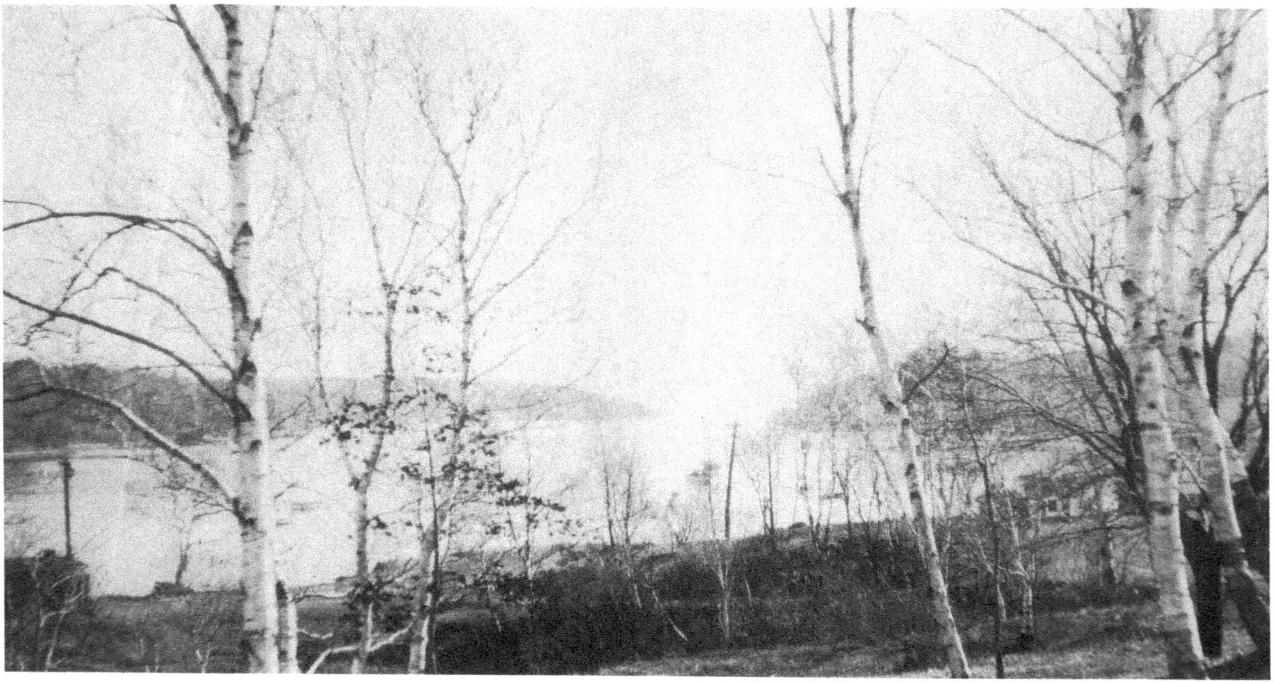

Northwest Arm of Halifax Harbour

his house. By a trick of memory, I have recalled his unusual Lunenburg county surname for a lifetime.

When we got to the gates, it was somewhat shocking to see that ordinary, everyday life went on as usual, ignoring our holiday. A steady stream of trucks, cars and delivery vehicles — milk, ice, mail, coal — was steaming in both directions along Purcell's Cove Road. We were back in the real world.

Thus, at age seven or eight, I was exposed to the charms of this special place. I knew and felt its appeal long before I could try to articulate it.

Always pressed for time in the morning, we hardly ever walked through the Dingle on the way to school. In the three and a half years I attended Cunard School, I probably walked there fewer than three and a half times. (The half occasion was when the bus broke down near the Dingle gates, and we had to go on foot the rest of the way.) But a few of the boys made it a point, except in bitter mid-winter, to walk home through the Dingle now and then.

That holy place hardly ever changed. The tower was always the same, and the lions, the wavelets, the bandstand, the squirrels and Mrs. Schmeisser, after we learned to give back her friendly wave when she spotted us through her kitchen window. There was an endless supply of young mothers pushing their perambulators and strollers. And then, on one of the most memorable days of my young childhood, something shocking was different.

Approaching the tower from the paved road that curved below it, we ran up the granite steps and —

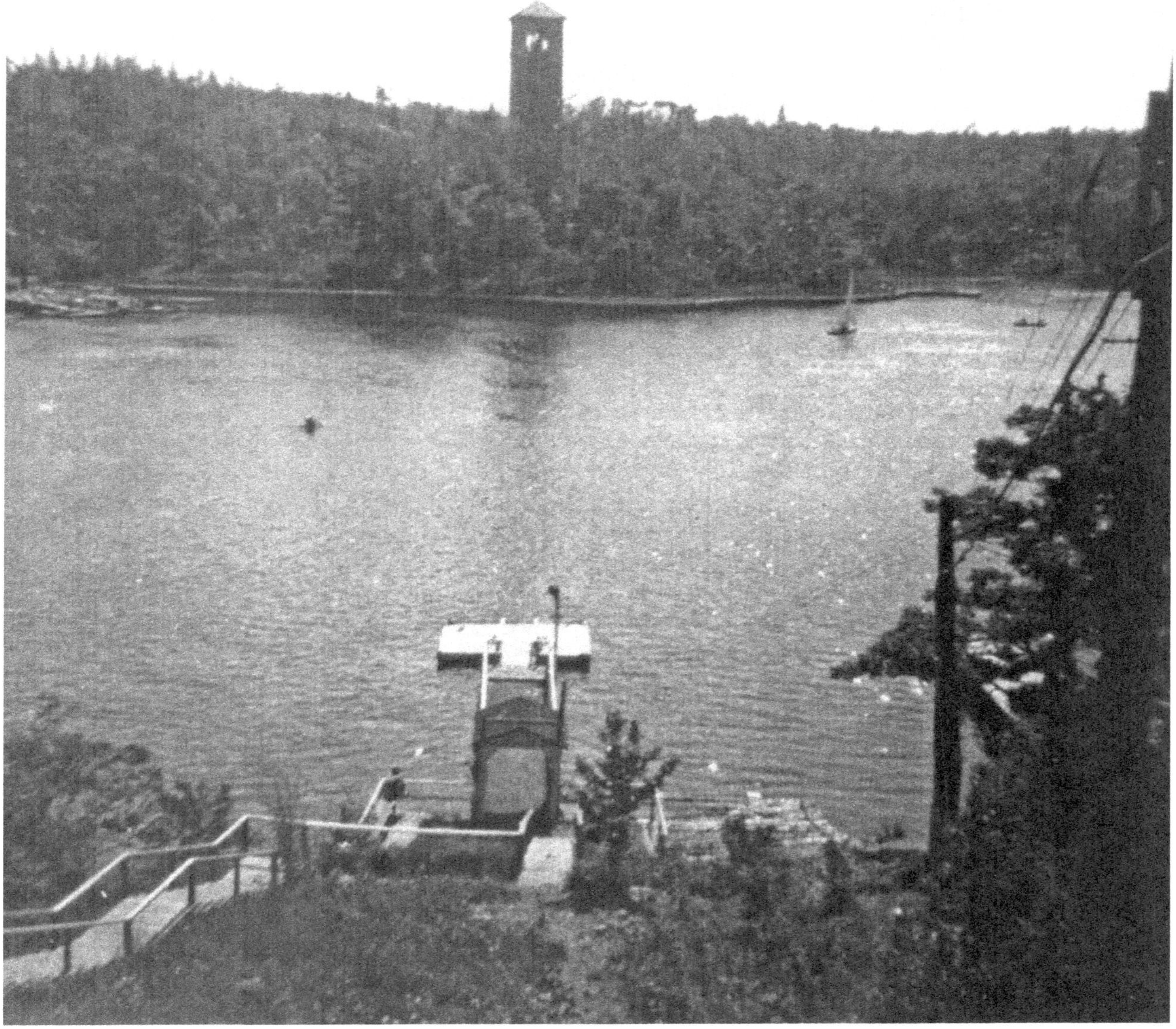

Wharf for Oakland Road ferry

the main doors were gaping wide open! At 3 p.m. on a weekday, this was unprecedented. We ran inside. There were no grown-ups in sight. The floor above was reached by a circular metal staircase. From there, the open tower reached high above us, beckoning. Everything echoed, and there were still no adults.

Stairs were attached to the inside of the tower's outer walls with bolts strong enough, one hopes, to last forever, since the stairs had and have no other means of support. They made about two turns around the tower as they spiralled up through the gloom. Above the first landing, things became dangerous. When we leaned over the railing, we were peering straight down twenty, fifty, eventually eighty feet to the first storey's steel ceiling. Now one more circular staircase brought us to open air at the top. The viewing platform, which extended around the tower's whole circumference, was bounded by an outer wall, which we just managed to see over.

Whooping and hollering no doubt, we ran around the complete circuit, taking in the scene in all directions, and excitedly pointing out what we could see. Below and beyond a grove of trees — we were looking over the tops of them — lay the village of Jollimore. There was the clearing that marked the location of our school and its playground. The wave-flecked, turquoise Northwest Arm stretched below the seaward side of the tower, with the elegant South End of Halifax on the other side. Towards the park gates lay the curving seawall, the pathed lawn and bandstand and — emerging from behind the bandstand, a long-legged, running figure! It was Mr. Schmeisser. As he covered ground at an amazing speed, he was waving in our direction and shouting something. Although we could not make out the exact words, we could guess the general idea.

The tower was too tall for us to get freely away. We were halfway to the bottom when we met Mr. Schmeisser coming up. He spoke to us sternly, told us to keep out of the tower and advised us to keep away from the railing and stay against the wall as we descended on this, our last, visit.

At the time this incident happened, I thought it was about the misbehaviour of schoolboys. I see now, of course, that it was about the groundskeeper, who had neglected to keep the tower locked up. How his heart must have fluttered and stopped, ice-cold, when he heard distant hollering and, fingering in his overalls pocket the key with which he had unlocked the tower doors, saw our little heads gaily bobbing at the top of that dangerous pinnacle. With what powerful dread and guilt did he bound towards disaster as it unfolded. And then, what relief, to find that none of us had fallen off.

CHAPTER 6 1942–45

Second World War

I remember World War II. Actually, I do not remember a whole lot about the war. One recollection concerns going to the movies. It was in the afternoon, probably on a Saturday when Dad could be home with the twins. It was one of the movie houses on Barrington Street: the Orpheus, I think, not the Capitol. Three of us — Mother, my sister and me — joined a queue of a hundred souls waiting to get in. A photograph of this line-up would distinctively proclaim itself as a wartime shot. Every person on that straggling sidewalk was carrying an aluminum pot, pan or lid; that was the price of admission. The government was collecting scrap metal, to be melted down into airplanes or shell casings. People were probably advised to keep at least one pot, or pan, and to practise frying eggs in the same utensil that cooked the morning porridge. This might seem an unpalatable prospect, but we were too young to care. The movie was depressing too, a drama in the grimy context of ecological disaster in Wales, *How Green Was My Valley.*

I also remember rationing. The government was controlling the consumption of key commodities such as tea, sugar, butter and meat. Shoppers in grocery stores needed money to buy these things, but they also needed permission from the government. This came in the form of stamps, issued through the post office. Each stamp represented an okay, during a certain stretch of time, to purchase a set quantity of the restricted item. Basic amounts were approved for single adults. A couple with several young children qualified for quite a bit more. As the children grew older, more changes occurred. Mother carefully sorted through her ration booklets before setting out to the store.

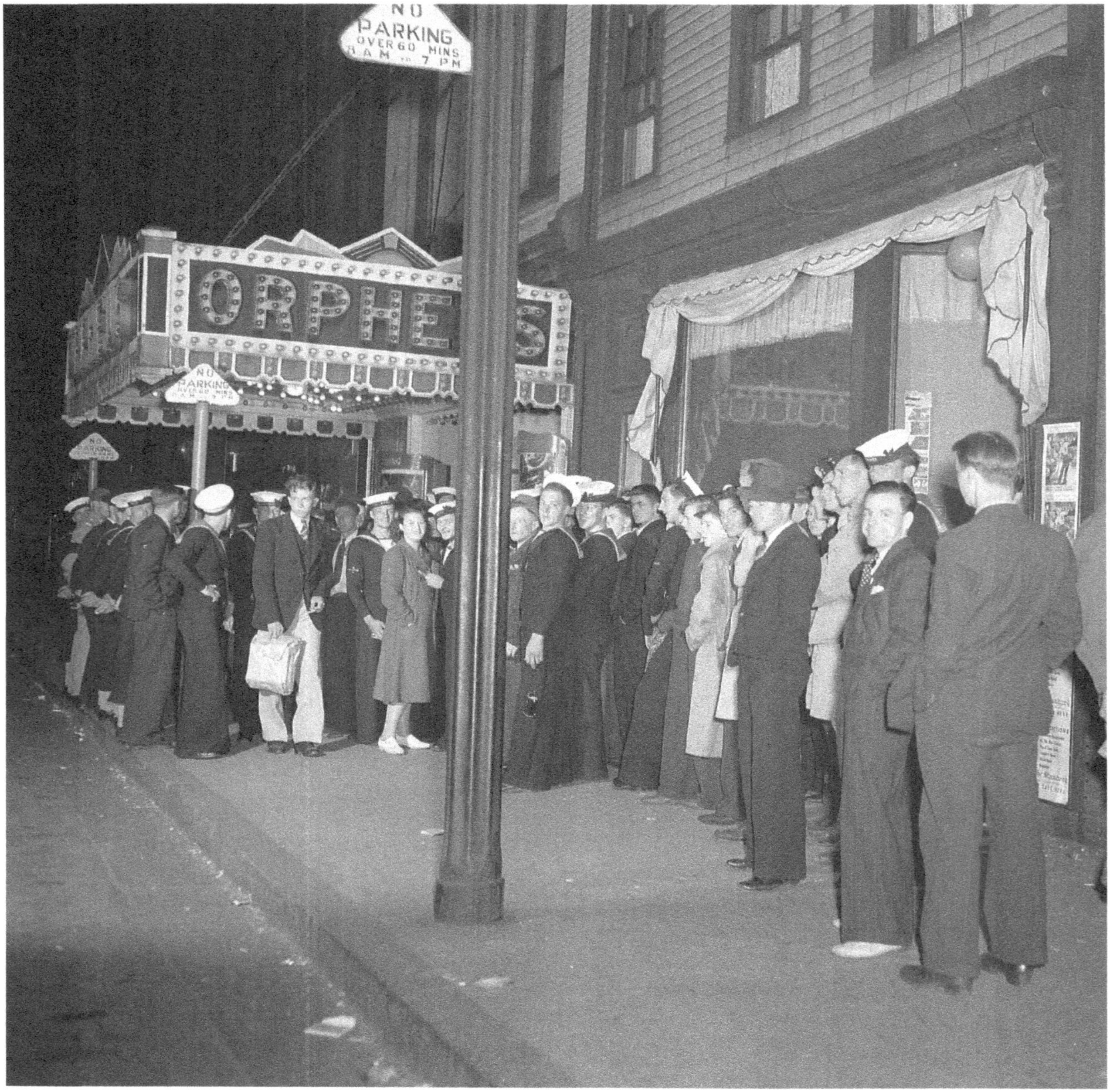

Orpheus theatre, Barrington Street

Neighbours no doubt traded stamps: Those who wanted more than their fair allotment of sugar could give up some meat to get it; the terms of such exchanges varied from one locality to the next.

Little children had their own war-inspired booklets. These were for war savings stamps, which represented receipts for a few pennies or a nickel brought to school to help win the war. The collection was taken on Fridays. Teacher would take my money and stick the proper stamp in the booklet, which went home in my bookbag. The stamps showed powerful images. I remember three of them — the Hitler, the Mussolini and the Tojo stamps. The familiar, oversized face of an enemy dictator — attached to a very miniscule body — was shown in the cockpit of an aircraft that was on fire and about to crash.

This program, aimed even at six-, seven- and eight-year-olds, is a sign of how very intimately intrusive and all-inclusive wartime propaganda was. The stamps' crude pictures appealed to the brutal nature of children. They seemed meant to make us rejoice in the imminent destruction of these evil persons and, if we thought the matter right through, whatever it was they stood for. It is not likely the government raised any revenue this way. Perhaps the money that came in more or less equalled the cost of printing and distributing the stamps. It seems to have been, at least chiefly, an effort in mind control and indoctrination.

It worked. Through my early childhood, I am sure I did not think anything on these political subjects except what the government told me to think. Ideas were planted — thick, solid, uncriticized certainties — that lasted long after the war ended. I was a young teenager before reaching the first stage of intellectual liberation, starting to think for myself. It was thanks to an enlightened Sunday school teacher.

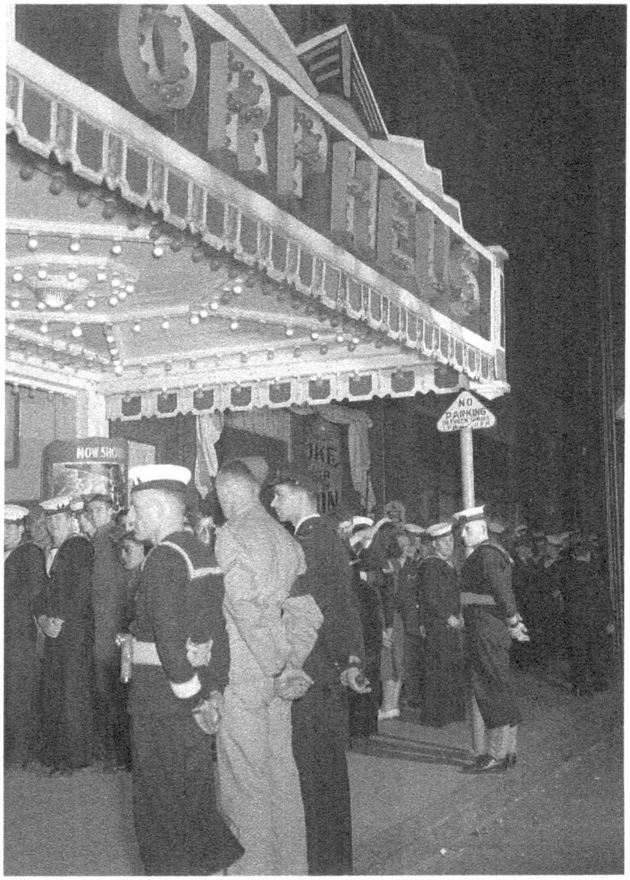

Orpheus theatre, Barrington Street

Mr. Ward challenged us to say something positive and praise the good or strong attributes of Adolf Hitler. This was subversive, and, we thought at first, impossible. To us, Hitler was the embodiment of everything evil and that was that. Mr. Ward, bless his persistent memory, would not let us off the hook. For instance, could Hitler read maps? Well, he seemed to direct a whole war on several fronts at once, so we reluctantly supposed that he could. Could he remember where all

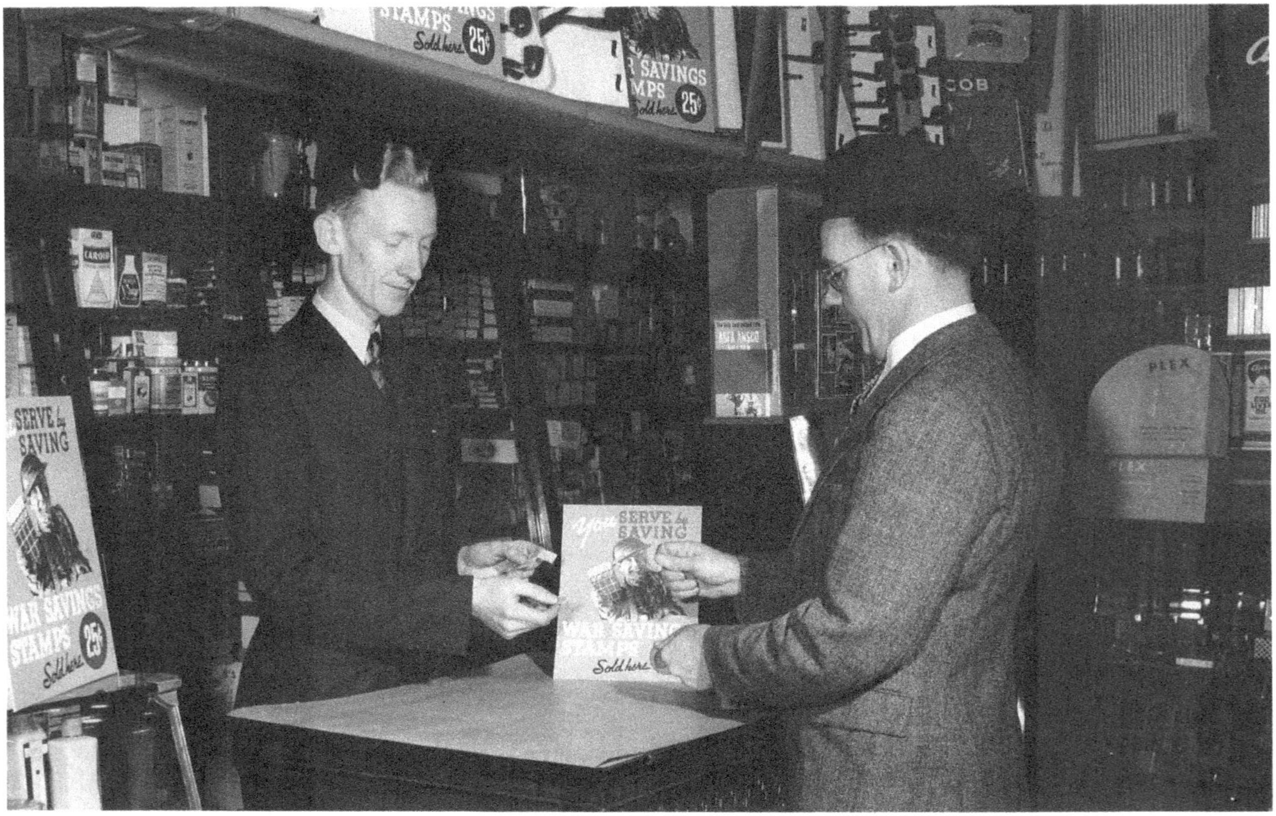

War savings stamps being purchased

those military units, with their various equipments and capabilities, were stationed? Hmmm. Apparently he could; that's pretty smart. Could Hitler drive a car? Judging by the newsreels we had seen, there was usually a chauffeur. Could he direct the affairs of a complicated government, so effectively that they almost won the war? Yes, yes, yes — by the end of that class, some of us were rapidly and excitedly unwriting the history of a crippling brainwashing that had been imposed on the generation of wartime children.

While it lasted, the Second World War reached to every aspect of developing personalities and shaped us quite thoroughly. It even directed our witticisms, which, seriously intended at the time, became cute sayings passed down in family folklore. My mother's warm, flamboyant younger sister used to babysit us. I naturally fell in love with her. I was eight. "Greta," I announced, "we should get married" — thoughtful pause — "but we'll have to wait until I am twelve, for that is when I'll get a tea ration."

CHAPTER 7 1932–42

Family

I was brought up in a family of six. There were, first of all, Dad and Mother, named Ian and Sadie. They were married in 1932, in the depth of the Great Depression, in the United Church at Mother's girlhood home: Grand River, near St. Peters, Richmond County, Cape Breton. My parents' wedding, I was told, was the first to take place in that new little church, which dates from 1928. My older sister and I were born, two years apart, in the mid 1930s. Five years later, just before victories at El Alamein and Stalingrad promised that the enemy might be defeated in World War II, the family was completed with the arrival of my two younger sisters, the twins.

Mother's personality and role provided the main glue that unified the family. She was an affectionate partner to Dad, and a constantly available, constantly supportive mentor and confidante to her children.

Her own upbringing at Grand River had occurred in an ethnically very interesting situation. In that part of Cape Breton, nearly the entire Atlantic coastline is a continuous string of francophone Acadian settlements. The interior, on the other hand, is just as fully monopolized by communities of Scots extraction — half Presbyterian, half Catholic — dating from Gaelic-speaking immigration from 1810 to the 1820s. When I was a boy visiting Cape Breton, I observed late stages of the process whereby the Scots became assimilated into the Canadian anglophone majority. I have heard my grandparents carry on conversations in Gaelic, but my own parents, never; as for me, I have just two or three words of that lost language.

In the simple sociology of Grand River, Mother belonged to a family that was — modestly — elite. Her father was a merchant. Grandpa operated one of only two general stores in the village. Most other families were in debt to him, running up charge accounts for groceries and supplies purchased at the store. Mother and her five siblings were all well educated, and one became a medical doctor.

Social leadership can, however, have its pitfalls. In 1925, when Mother was a teenager, major Protestant denominations combined to form the United Church of Canada. Whereas Methodists and Congregationalists were united supporting the project, many Presbyterian congregations split apart on the issue. Grandpa, a Presbyterian elder, was one of the leaders in the small group of families that left the traditional church and established a congregation of the United Church.

Now fast-forward a half-century ahead. Former teenager, now approaching age sixty-five, Mother applied for the Old Age Security pension. She was told to submit her birth certificate. When none was available, the bureaucrats said a baptism certificate would do as well. She contacted the Grand River Presbyterian church, only to learn that during the debate over church union, tempers had flared so badly that the records of families who left to form the United Church congregation had been deliberately burned.

In their lifetimes, Mother and her siblings were exposed to powerful forces promoting outmigration from the countryside, which transformed Canada through the mid-twentieth century. Demonstrating a typical scatter pattern, two moved to Ontario, one to Boston, and Mother and one other to the Halifax area, while only one brother remained behind and took over the store. While the cause of this urbanizing dispersion lies in powerful continental, even global, processes, in Mother's case it was very much in line with her individual preference as well. She often told us children how conscious she was, growing up, of the limitations and deprivations of rural living. For her own children, she early decided, she wanted the advantages of city life: stores, libraries, a wider range of friends and interests, cultural opportunities and easier access to college.

Another story she told us illustrated a Sadie-and-Ian split over the values of city life. Since she was of a poetic cast of mind, prone to embellishment, some parts of this story (perhaps the most interesting and major ones) may not be quite true. Nevertheless, as she told it, after they had been married two or three years, Dad was offered the chance to take over the family farm in Loch Lomond, and he apparently wanted to do so. According to Mother, she put her foot down. They had already moved from Halifax to Lunenburg, and she would not put up with any more rural-oriented backsliding. If compelled, as a dutiful wife, she would move with her husband to the backwoods of Loch Lomond, but there would be no more children. This, I eventually learned, was meant to be a euphemism for the message "No more sex." Marlene had been born at the time, but not me. This threat, therefore, if implemented, might have made this whole memoir redundant, or worse. I wish, though, that I had the chance to ask Dad for his version of the event.

Mother often discussed with us her theory or philosophy of parenting. This was based, but not modelled, on her girlhood experiences. She did not approve of her own mother's style of bringing up children; it was too regimented and dictatorial. The children's wishes and inclinations were never consulted. Instead, they were continually herded and ordered: where to go, what to wear, what to do, what to say, with no choices being presented. Whether Grandma was

Family

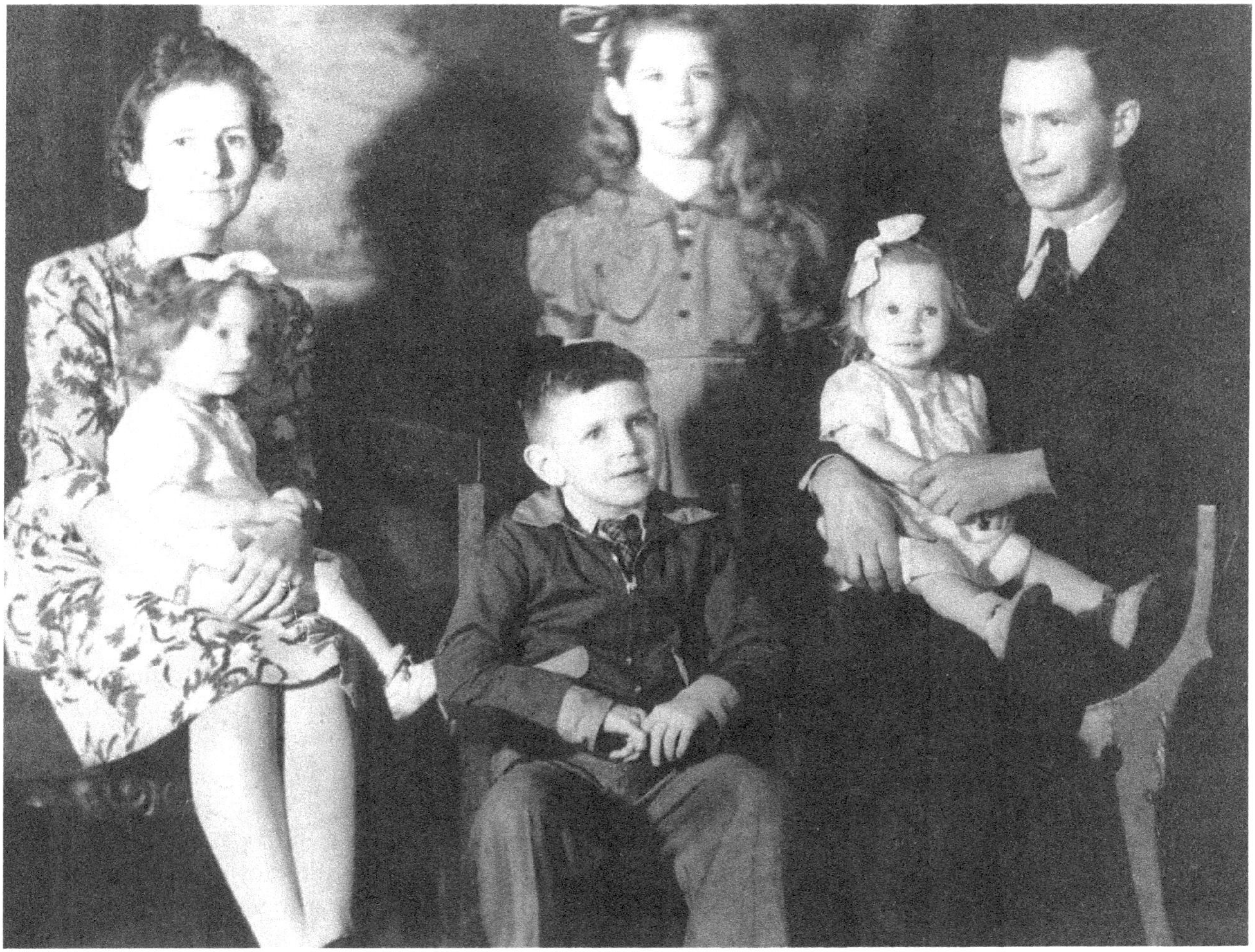

The family was completed when the twins were born. Sadie is holding Mora, Dad has Joan. The author, age 6, is front-centre. Marlene, behind me, is almost 9.

so indifferent to the children's wishes, as Mother seemed to recall, I cannot say. I knew Grandma as a feisty, loving old woman who could not wait to get the grandkids settled into their visit so that the endless game of Auction 45s could continue. That was Grandma in the relaxed mode of grandparenthood. Back in the days when she had six children coming along, at various stages of development, things would have been different. Perhaps she was often quite harried, too busy to listen.

At any rate, Mother explained, she resolved she would follow a parenting style opposite to her own mother's approach. She would never be too busy to listen, and never force the children to do anything they did not want to do. For example, she repeatedly told us, "You don't have to go to school if you don't want to." This was rather a risky message. As far as I know, my sisters and I were always happy enough to go to school. How Mother would have handled things if the contrary situation had arisen, she fortunately never had to find out.

For sharing her children's interests, giving weight to our wishes and sympathetically siding with us in the various vicissitudes of life, she was first rate. I remember an incident at age five, when I threw a stone back at a boy who was throwing stones at me. I got him on the face. Soon his mother was at our door complaining. "Malcolm is sorry," said Mother, "and he is being punished. I am keeping him indoors." Actually, she fully understood, and supported, my need to defend myself. She spun that story about keeping me in for the sake of peace in the neighbourhood. Meanwhile, my "punishment" consisted of staying away from the windows, so the neighbours couldn't watch as I snacked on cookies and milk, and started work in a new colouring book that Mother had stored somewhere, ready for a special occasion.

After I grew up, I found that many of the people I encountered had complaints or unresolved issues about how badly their own parents has treated them in childhood. I harboured no such resentments. Later she proved to be a somewhat difficult in-law, but in my boyhood years, I found her unfailingly available to advise, to warn, to encourage and to understand.

There is one other aspect of her personality that needs to go into this record. She was a very literate person, fond of reading and of discussing what she read. She had a lifelong habit of committing to memory long swathes of verse: Browning, Tennyson, Housman, Hopkins. As children, we admired and copied this inclination. She also wrote quite a bit of poetry herself. From girlhood she was always composing verses, short and pithy, triggered by particular events and observations. Grandma scolded her when she found these efforts in Mother's school notebooks; perhaps she ripped the pages out. To Grandma, Mother said, writing poetry was a bad habit, like chewing gum. Only a little of her verse was ever published — a few pieces in the daily newspaper, and more in annual chapbooks of the Nova Scotia Poetry Society, of which she was a member for many years. When Mother was about eighty, I collected and re-typed most of her poetry, and put it together in a sixty-page looseleaf binder. This act of filial piety is one of the good things I have done in my lifetime; I am glad I thought of it.

Some of her nicest short verses are well calculated to bring a lump to the throat, waterworks not excluded. For example, after one of the twins asked a provocative question, Mother wrote

How high do I reach? my little girl asked,
Standing on tiptoe with care.
My darling, I answered, You reach to my heart,
And I keep you there.

Or, this one, which she wrote for me while I was at graduate school in Toronto:

His toys! He's left them, call him back!
He will need them in his play.
Dreaming mother, don't you know?
He's grown up and gone away.

In guiding my early and middle boyhood, Dad was less significant than Mother. Mind you, he was a very good father — patient, hardly ever angry, an excellent model of the hard-working head of household. Though he did not say so, I never had any doubt that he was well satisfied with me and the way I was turning out. For occasions when Dad had to reprove me, a careful formula evolved. He would say: "For a smart boy, Malcolm, you can certainly do some dumb things." I must have heard that a dozen times growing up. Notice the messages contained in that form of words. I am not a bad boy; I am not even dumb. Although smart, I was, however, capable of making mistakes.

Dad contrasted greatly with Mother in that he did not share in our daily little woes and triumphs. His lack of conversation with the children was most glaringly revealed when Mother kept my older sister out of school for several consecutive weeks. Eventually, a nosy neighbour alerted Dad to the situation. Apparently, he never asked Marlene, "What did you do in school today?" It was Mother, too, who responded to and encouraged our developing interests, even masculine ones. When, at age ten, I became a passionate baseball fan, she took me to see my first real game — an outing complete with my first hamburger. When I became a high school basketball star, I remember her at one or two of the games, but Dad, never.

Why was he so, apparently, distant? Well, he was busy. He could not easily take time off in the middle of the day. His job sometimes took him out of town for three or four days at a time. Until I was seventeen, we had no car, so he was late moving into the role of chauffeur-confidante, common in many families when the kids rely on Dad for transportation. More important, probably, was the spirit of the time. In the 1940s and 1950s, division of labour in families declared wives responsible for bringing up the children. Then ideas and patterns changed. With my own son, in the 1970s and 1980s, I was much more of a hands-on parent than my father had been. In the early twenty-first century, my son shares with his wife — shares equally, as far as I can tell — all the jobs and joys of parenting. It would be unfair to declare Dad's detachment from childish concerns to be an error or weakness according to standards that developed only after his children were grown.

Dad came from a background quite different than Mother's. She was a child of the countryside: small-scale everything, few neighbours, no electricity or running water. Dad, however, grew up in a citadel of small-town sophistication: Sussex, New Brunswick. With its population of several thousand, Sussex was an important station on the Saint John–Moncton railway, and functioned as service centre and supply depot for the dairyland of southeastern New Brunswick. Sussex High School was a magnet attracting ambition from all the surrounding countryside; the town was the seat of administration for the county municipality and location of a large World War I army camp. Thus, while Mother may sometimes have felt a hick out of place in the metropolis, Dad was accustomed to living at the centre of important activities.

One of the businesses that contributed to the bustle of Sussex was the newspaper *The Maritime Farmer*, an influential bi-weekly owned by the Saint John *Telegraph-Journal* and edited by Dad's father, Malcolm MacLeod. Editor MacLeod was the grandfather we never knew, since he died young. He travelled the Maritimes drumming up interest in his newspaper, judging exhibits at farm fairs and keeping in touch with agricultural societies. At home, he wrote and edited copy extolling the rural lifestyle. He was closely linked to the New Brunswick provincial government, and briefly served as deputy minister of agriculture. Headed by such a regional celebrity, Dad's family was of elite status in the Sussex context — but not so elite as it would have been if they had owned instead of merely edited the paper.

Dad had an amazing range of skills that made him the complete do-it-yourselfer. As a trained electrician, he could do wiring. He did plumbing too, soaking up what he needed to learn as he went along. He successfully tackled projects in landscaping, gardening and septic arrangements. With telephone company climbing gear, he went to the top of the tallest trees installing the aerial for his amateur radio station. Single-handedly — except for the little help I was able to give him around age eleven or twelve — he transformed a one-storey house with a steep roof into a nearly flat-roofed home of two storeys, creating four additional bedrooms. Observing all this work, I was greatly impressed and learned many valuable lessons — especially, to be triply cautious when using dynamite to shatter huge granite boulders into pieces of manageable weight.

Dad never talked much. His mother died when he was seven. Did he preserve any memories of her? He never said. Later another woman, brave enough to take on the task of raising five children not her own, entered the family. Was it easy, or even possible, to accept her authority as substitute mother? He never said. After Marlene was born, did he really want to give up his job with the Maritime Telegraph and Telephone Company and take up hard-scrabble farming on stony acres in Loch Lomond? He never said.

So, I may not fully understand some of the aspects and angles of my parents' experience, especially Dad's.

Moving to the next generation of our little family, I have to say I consider myself an expert on the subject of sisters. I survived a boyhood, after all, growing up with three of them — with no brothers for buffers. Here is the conclusion I have reached: Sisters are great!

If they catch you young enough, they will paint all your twenty nails with polish of various colours. There is really nothing much you can do about it (except lick it off, all but the cherry-coloured ones). On other occasions, they will let you show them how to hammer the other kind of nail into a log, stick or, parents being away, wall. Of course, parents eventually come home. Forever after, for a lifetime, you can hear the sweet soprano voices of the sisters singing in cruel chorus, "HE did it!"

An older sister will take you to a birthday party where they dance. This puts you several steps of sophistication ahead of most of your Grade 7 friends, who are still playing with slinkies. Shimmy trumps slinky. Younger sisters will let you lug their pillow cases packed with assorted Halloween loot up the heavy hill towards home. Having abandoned childish trick-or-treat, you happened to meet them struggling when you were going out to practise your latest dance steps. Half the load was jelly beans. They let you have the cherry ones.

My older sister, Marlene, was a constant companion in my earliest years. She recalls, better than I do, interesting talks we used to have when I was ten and she twelve and we slept in side-by-side cots in an unfinished, unheated attic. "Unfinished" means that nails holding on the roofing protruded down through the overhead boards. "Unheated" means that in winter, these tips of nails turned white with frost. This was before Dad raised the roof and made separate, comfortable bedrooms up there.

For a long time, into adulthood, I made the mistake of thinking I was smarter than Marlene. This was the result of Mother over-stressing the fact that I often led the class in elementary school. Also, Marlene used to discuss her schoolwork with Mother and would even accept suggestions for good lines she could use in her compositions; while I preferred to work more independently. When Marlene was at Nova Scotia Normal College after finishing Grade 12, she won the Governor General's medal as the outstanding all-round student and student leader. Smart as I allegedly was, I never won so prestigious an award.

Marlene also remembers more clearly than I do the quarrels we used to have while working side by side on the dishes, taking turns to wash or to dry. The fights meant more to her than to me, probably because she had a common, standard problem: the first child's jealousy of a new baby coming along and drawing away much of the available attention. One of the cute stories about Marlene, when she was still being socialized into language, reveals this jealousy. I was about one, she was three. For the first time, I grabbed the bars of my crib and hoisted myself onto my legs. Marlene happily ran to give Mother the long-awaited good news: "Mommy, Mommy, she's going, she's going!"

When the twins were born, I took almost as much pride in the accomplishment as my parents did. Ordinary families had babies one at a time, but we were special. On the very day the little bundles came home from the hospital, Mother threw challenges. Would I show I was ready to love them, by kissing their bare little bottoms? When I passed that test, she asked if, being five and a half years older, I would help to protect and bring them up? I was a serious-minded little fellow, and soberly took on the responsibility of being an additional parent.

Marlene and I indeed helped bring them up — Marlene more than me, I think, she being another girl. When we reached proper babysitting ages, and Mother was leaving us in charge, her last words often were: "Now Marlene, Malcolm, I expect you to amuse the twins." As soon as she was gone, those littlest angels would plant themselves in front of us, tilt their twin grins up expectantly and say: "You have to 'muse us."

After the children were grown, Mother used to say she thought the twins had a more advantaged upbringing than the older children did. What she had in mind was the fact that Dad's salary grew during those years. For the twins, the family could afford extra expenses like ballet and figure skating lessons, while Marlene and I had not had similar opportunities. I assured Mother she had nothing at all to apologize for; we felt in no way deprived.

In fact the twins — being junior, and forming a sort of two-for-one package — probably suffered somewhat at times when it was difficult for them to have each of their separate needs and personalities fully recognized. Whereas Marlene and I had our own private bedrooms, the twins shared. When I was between seven and nine years old, we lived right on the shore of the Northwest Arm, and had a little rowboat for short excursions. Mother, the poet in the family, named this craft. It was the MARMAC J: MAR for Marlene and MAC for me — three letters each — while Joan and Judith Mora, the twins who could not yet swim or row, had to settle for one lonely, tacked-on J shared between them.

Luckily, after Dad retired, he became more reflective and chatty, and I perhaps more persistent in questioning. During that closing stage of his life, I finally heard several good stories that helped me know him better. The story I like best concerned how he met Mother.

After Dad finished high school, he spent a year or more operating the otherwise-unoccupied family farm in Loch Lomond with his older brother Bill. They also had the contract for collecting outgoing mail at several points, lugging it out to the highway, picking up the new mail and distributing it around. Due to this twice-daily tour of the whole community, Dad was first among all the young men of Loch Lomond, potential suitors, to learn that the new teacher — Sadie Cameron of Grand River — had arrived. She was boarding with a certain family. By a suspiciously coincidental turn of fortune, that evening after supper, Dad happened to hitch up the buggy and make a social call at that very home. The whole family was gathered in the kitchen for Presbyterian devotions. Dad sat on the couch next to the new teacher. When the grandfather turned from Bible-reading to prayer, everyone kneeled. Without interrupting the prayer, Dad was able to whisper, "Will you go for a drive?"

Mother's answer deserves to be blazoned at the head of this chapter, or more likely at the very front of everything, since it became the foundation and trigger for the whole story I am telling in this book. She said "Yesss."

CHAPTER 8 1946—50

Kline Heights

From the head of the Northwest Arm, follow Herring Cove Road uphill. Keep right where Purcell's Cove Road branches off, and right again at the corner where Bedley's store stood in the 1940s. The street you have located is Withrod Drive. When it starts climbing quite steeply, you are entering the area known as Kline Heights.

When I lived there, Kline Heights was a residential district consisting of Withrod Drive and a dozen or so streets that branched off it on one side or the other. There was no direct link to Spryfield. The built-up area petered out before reaching Long Lake and other parts of the Halifax city water supply. In that backwoods country, there was also a Withrod Lake in which, according to one of Mother's fanciful stories, the young son in a family was drowned. In her grief, the mother decided to end her now-empty life in the same lake, leaving behind a note, "I am going to be with Rod."

Leaving romanticized notions aside, the area of Kline Heights was a bedroom suburb for Halifax, not very well planned and, at that time, lacking water and sewer services. It was home to the working poor — families headed by stevedores were common — and to aspiring middle class folks like ourselves. Within sight from our new address were a couple of homes still partially clad in black tar paper. They remained that way for a year or two, until the families got sufficient funds ahead to proceed to the next stage of construction. The Heights was saved from slum status, however, by lack of crowding. It was a democracy of little homes: Almost every place was a single-family dwelling.

Populated by honest, hard-working folk, the Heights certainly had its share of problems. Our steep street was never plowed in the winter (to my way of thinking, not really a problem but an advantage: great for coasting). In the neighbourhood we had a woman who eventually committed suicide. Next door to us, there was a husband and father who sometimes became an over-friendly, foolish drunk on weekends. Across the street, when we moved there, was a man who drank much too much, weekend or not. I remember the shouting and swearing, the sound of glass breaking and him writhing on the ground outside his house, yelling and screaming until the ambulance arrived. At a tender age, I learned the phrase delirium tremens (DTs). Still, the area definitely did not deserve the reputation enshrined in the old joke, which I nevertheless enjoyed repeating, "No, I'm not afraid of heights" — strategic pause — "except Kline Heights." In all the years we lived there, the afternoon of the DTs is the only time I remember seeing a police car on our little street.

The summer I was nine years old, between grades 4 and 5, we moved from Melville Cove to Kline Heights. It was only a short distance, about a half a mile by road, much less if you cut through backyards. It meant, however, that in the fall, we had to search for new friends in a new school. It was not very difficult. On my first morning in Grade 5, I sat next to another boy on a two-person bench with a common desktop. I asked permission to sharpen my pencil, did so, and returned to my seat. In the general excitement prevailing — I seem to have been waving my arms around, still holding the pencil — I managed to stab Albert in the cheek, just below the eye. Parents hate this kind of thing. Boys don't really mind; they understand. This unusual icebreaker was the introduction to a friendship that lasted a lifetime.

For a brief transitional period, we gravitated between the old place and the new. I remember being deposited by car at the ball field near Melville Island prison. I had my softball glove, and joined friends from the old neighbourhood in the usual Saturday afternoon ball game. After dropping my usual quota of easy fly balls, I walked up the foreign hill to the new home.

Our cat, Washtubs (Washie), went back too. On a couple of occasions when she did not come home overnight, Dad went down to the Cove and found her prowling around the doors, once so friendly, now mysteriously shut and barred to her.

We walked back and forth to school four times a day, coming home for lunch. Usually we followed the roads, but in the winter, frozen Chocolate Lake often became an alternate route for the first part of the homeward trek. Directly across the Purcell's Cove and Herring Cove Road intersection from South Armdale School, the lake stretched for about a half a mile, getting more narrow in its farthest reach. Chocolate Lake was located in Armdale proper, not in Kline Heights. Nevertheless, it was on the way to the Heights if we chose to go that way; and more importantly, during the frozen half of the school year, it became our principal playground.

At the lake's near end, water moving rapidly towards the spillway created a section of thin ice and then permanently open water. We were fortunate, however, in never having anyone go through the ice there. Apparently everybody was wise enough to avoid the dangerous section.

Unless snow-covered, most of Chocolate Lake was great for skating. On late afternoons and weekends, it accommodated plenty of athletes and lookers-on: little kids pushing chairs, still learning; parents picking them up; girls trying to twirl; every boy with a hockey stick in hand.

We had very challenging games on that ice. It was not what could be called organized hockey. At each end of a designated area, a homely pair of ordinary boots served as goalposts. There was a rule against lifting the puck, but it could never be enforced. The worst thing was, there were no sideboards. Every so often, due to an errant pass or shot, lifted or not, the puck would escape from the game. Down the ice it would go, bouncing over ridges and rough spots, perhaps all the way to the distant shoreline. Someone, usually the youngest or most vulnerable player, would be deputized to go on the long skate and get it back. Meanwhile, the others rested.

These games were a meeting place where boys from our side of the lake met those from the other (St. Margaret's Bay Road) side, who often attended different schools. One of the boys I casually encountered in this fashion was later a long-serving mayor of Halifax. He ran the city the same way he played hockey: with a lot of momentum.

On winter evenings, Chocolate Lake was magically transformed. There were a couple of skate-houses where Keddy's Motel was later built (later a Best Western). They were heated places with benches where you could lace on your skates, a snack bar at one end and music blaring outside. An oval-shaped area of ice in front of the skatehouses was always kept cleared of snow. Here, when we were thirteen and fourteen, we had our first little dates.

A daring fellow would emerge from the pack of boys on one side of the oval, go over to the girls and ask one of them to go for a skate. Hand in hand — or, I preferred, arm in arm — they would take a few turns around the ice, thank each other and go back to gossip with their friends. In the second stage of this dating technique, such couples left the well-lit area to skate the full length of the lake. This was very romantic: bright moonlight, Bing Crosby's crooning from the loudspeakers getting more and more faint, nobody else around, and a few rough spots on the ice that made partners grip each other more tightly. When they got back to the lighted oval, there would invariably be jokes and jeers about how long they were gone. This was our adolescent version of "going all the way" — that is, going all the way down the lake.

Kline Heights, and the routes leading to it, are where we had our most formative experiences — as the song has it, "skinned our hearts and skinned our knees." Forty years after leaving home, one of my sisters and I went back to see the old homestead, now in the possession of others. One of these kind strangers invited us in to look things over. My room, which had been very small as a bedroom, was now an oversized, say gigantic, bathroom. Two of the other bedrooms had been made into one long one — with a skylight! As some people find, you can't go home again. Perhaps you can't even find it. The last time I drove up Kline Heights, so much had changed — streets widened and straightened after sewer pipes went in, sidewalks installed, shrubs grown into trees — that I did not recognize the strange place where Washie is buried in the backyard, until my sister said, "Stop, dummy, you just passed it!"

CHAPTER 9 1947–48

Movie Club

In the immediate post-war period, the spirit of the times insisted that assemblages of children be kept in strict and quiet order. For example: A teacher at South Armdale in that era recalls the school's morning routine. The first bell meant that children should be in their proper rooms. At the second bell, teachers followed them. When teacher entered the room, members of the class stood in the aisle by their desks and (singsongy) returned the standard greeting, "Good morning, Mr. G." Children were similarly herded and kept in order in Sunday school and other church- and community-oriented groupings. This chapter, however, recalls and celebrates the only regularly scheduled occasion on which children were able to slip the surly bonds of adult control and supervision. This happy freedom came at the Saturday morning movie club.

In my lifetime, I have been in some very noisy places. I have been in the attic with heavy thunder shouting just above the chimney-tops. I have been in front of the amplifiers at a rock concert. I have been near naval guns firing. But there was never a situation so full of bustle and noise, dancing all the decibels right off the scale, as the racket made by several hundred members of the Oxford Theatre Movie Club just before the show started on a Saturday morning.

When I was a schoolboy, the Oxford Theatre occupied the southwest corner of the strategic Quinpool Road and Oxford Street intersection. It still does — a tribute to good management. Back in the late 1940s, part of the Oxford's business plan was to maximize use of its expensive facilities and equipment. There were matinee and evening performances; now what about the mornings? Drawing a crowd to the theatre on weekday mornings apparently defeated them, but on Saturdays: ah-ha! The children were not in school. Thus was born the Oxford Theatre Movie Club.

Once launched, the club was advertised chiefly by word of mouth. The cost to belong was very small. But still, if you attracted a sufficient number of girls and boys, did not hire a squad of ushers to keep them in line — and did not mind the huge commotion they made when gathered into a confined space without much adult supervision — a profit could be squeezed out of Saturday morning, from ten to noon.

Picture me, then, leaving the house about nine o'clock and calling for my friend Albert a few doors down the hill. We were between ten and twelve years old. We walked on down to the Arm, where the rotary was later built. Now we had a choice to make. It was not between walking and public transit, for we always walked. Our question was: Shall we go by surface streets, or by the railway tracks? Usually we headed up Chebucto Road as far as the railway overpass, clambered up the embankment, and proceeded into town alongside the tracks. Or, more likely, on the tracks: walking on the rails, balancing, or stepping on each railway tie, or each second one, as the mood seized us. We were boys, and there was still a good half-hour before we had to be at the theatre.

After a quarter-mile of this unnecessarily energetic progress, the land rose around both sides of the rail line. The tracks now entered a tunnel-like ravine, cut through shale below city streets, which prevented the railway from interfering with the movement of motor vehicle traffic. All the way to the south end marshalling yard and station, streets cross on bridges overhead. Quinpool itself, after running parallel with the tracks for a good distance, takes a curve to the left, mounts a slope and is the first such street to cross. This is where we get off. Having climbed an embankment to get on the tracks, we now climbed again to exit, and continued like normal, civilized walkers another eight or ten blocks to the theatre.

When we get there, the place is in an uproar. From all over Halifax, from the closer parts of the county and even Dartmouth (while we took the train, sort of, they came by ferry), parents have exported family problems and babysitting chores to this one location. A harried young man named Leo is trying, failing, to keep order. Whether he was the theatre manager, or merely did not duck quickly enough when responsibility for Saturday morning movie club was assigned, we never found out.

Everyone is talking, except for those who are whistling, or singing country songs while strumming imaginary guitars. Some of the club members are friends who have not seen each other since last Saturday. They came in different groups from different directions, and are unfortunately located at opposite corners of the theatre. They shout greetings and news back and forth anyway. In this din, normal conversation is not possible. The din has therefore to increase, as you adjust your volume to scream remarks at point-blank range, right into your companion's poor ear.

Patrolling the aisles while seats fill up, Leo keeps good natured through all this trial. From time to time, groups of voices sing out, "Good morning, Leo," mocking the contrast between this bedlam and the orderliness of school. Usually Leo says the show cannot begin until there is quiet; everyone ignores that. He has a few other lines; the one I remember was to the effect that he was forming a young mother's club. Girls who wanted to be young mothers should see him after the show. Some of our girl chums who at eleven or twelve showed signs of development may have tittered at this. I apparently realized the scandalous implications of his remark, since I remember it. But my main effort was focussed, like Bugs Bunny, on singing, "On with the show!"

This is it! Leo has retreated to wherever managers go, the lights are dimmed, the screen starts flickering. First we have three or four cartoons. No Bugs Bunny, however. Bugs, Mickey and Donald were recent creations at that time, and in colour, therefore expensive and too good for the Saturday movie club crowd. Our cartoons were other cat-and-mouse dramas, old, black-and-white, grainy pictures with scratchy soundtracks. We give these cartoons the compliment of belly laughs anyway, while anticipating the morning's main feature, children's cinema, coming next.

Children's cinema at the Oxford Theatre Movie Club was not like *Harry Potter* or *Mary Poppins*, sentimental and slick. Rather, it was that study in ongoing suspense and surprise known as the serial. Some of these adventure stories kept going all winter. There were various types of serials: cops and robbers, for example, and cowboys and Indians. My personal favourite was jungle adventures. Although locations and costumes changed, all the stories followed the same, lock-step pattern. At the end of each hour-long episode, the hero had gotten himself into such a terrible predicament there was no way he could survive the death-dealing danger that was rushing upon him. He was plunging into a steaming vat of boiling water, or falling from a helicopter, or helplessly tied to railway tracks as a locomotive sped towards him.

Theatre lights come on, the club is over, see you next week. We knew the hero would be saved, but how? It turned out that, at the last second, if he were

- tied to tracks, the locomotive was switched to a different siding.
- falling from helicopter, he had a bullwhip at his belt with which he snagged a ride until he was able to drop into the refuse heap outside the next factory they passed over. (The factory manufactured feather pillows, giving him a soft landing.)
- in a vat of boiling water, it turned out the steam came from water that was excessively cold rather than hot. Luckily, our hero was invigorated by this plunge. He sprang out with such redoubled energy he was able to biff all the bad guys, seize back the stolen property and leer at the scantily-clad jungle girl (we did not really know why) all at the same time.

Those lucky outcomes, however, were for next week. On this Saturday noontime, we crowd out of the Oxford, blinking repeatedly at how bright it is outside. As we turn our steps towards home, we try to guess how the hero will get out of the fix he was in when he was last seen. We rarely guess right. Who could have anticipated a factory making feather pillows?

When we get to the spot where Quinpool crosses the rail line, we invariably scramble down to the tracks. We need the privacy, away from normal sidewalks, to fix in memory the film we have just seen. Without drawing disapproving stares from adult passersby, we can reenact key scenes from the serial. As we follow the rail line, there will be nobody to object to the whooping and hollering that will no doubt be required. We keep moving along, impelled by approaching lunchtime, but as we do, we dodge bullets, spears and arrows; fall down dead to confuse the enemy; steer commandeered vehicles screechingly around corners; blow things up; and, perennial favourite, make progress by swinging from imaginary vines.

When we get to the Chebucto Road overpass, lunch is more and more urgently calling for active, growing boys. We speed up the familiar roads and soon get home.

When I go into the house, the twins are arguing about something, both their cats are meowing, my other sister is practising an instrument and Mother is calling through the open back door to Dad who, in his lengthy landscaping project, is using a pneumatic drill on one of the granite boulders left by the last ice age. Refuge from another ear-challenging Saturday at the Oxford Theatre Movie Club, I think to myself, I love this peace and quiet.

CHAPTER 10 1948—54

Black and White

As a white child living on the outskirts of Halifax in the middle of the twentieth century, I had a somewhat racist upbringing.

Mind you, all the fully articulated ideas about race relations that were directed our way favoured the idea that in all essential respects, white and black people were similar and equal. We certainly heard this in church, at Bethany United on Dutch Village Road, where the minister frequently referred to the subject. His message was that attitudes favouring one race over another were unfair prejudice, based on incorrect information and sinful. We had occasional lessons in school, I think, leading to the same conclusions. My parents were fair-minded people of liberal enlightenment; they never uttered any suggestion of racial prejudice.

During all my formative years, in fact, I remember hearing only one statement that was blatantly racist, and it came from my own dear grandmother. Visiting her married daughters in Halifax, she was at our place after spending a few days on Duffus Street in Halifax's North End. This occurred before Africville was destroyed. Grandma told us that while she was sitting on the front porch on Duffus Street, a couple of black people — she would have said niggers — came strolling by. "Talking and laughing," she said, "walking along the sidewalk, just as if they were as good as anybody else." Young as I was, I heard the ignorance in her voice. I also forgave it — after all, Grandma lived in the deepest heart of Cape Breton Island, had hardly ever visited Sydney or anywhere else, and these may well have been the first black people she ever saw.

Few — besides Grandma — were advocating racism, but there was still plenty of it around. Frequent exhortations to avoid racial prejudice alerted

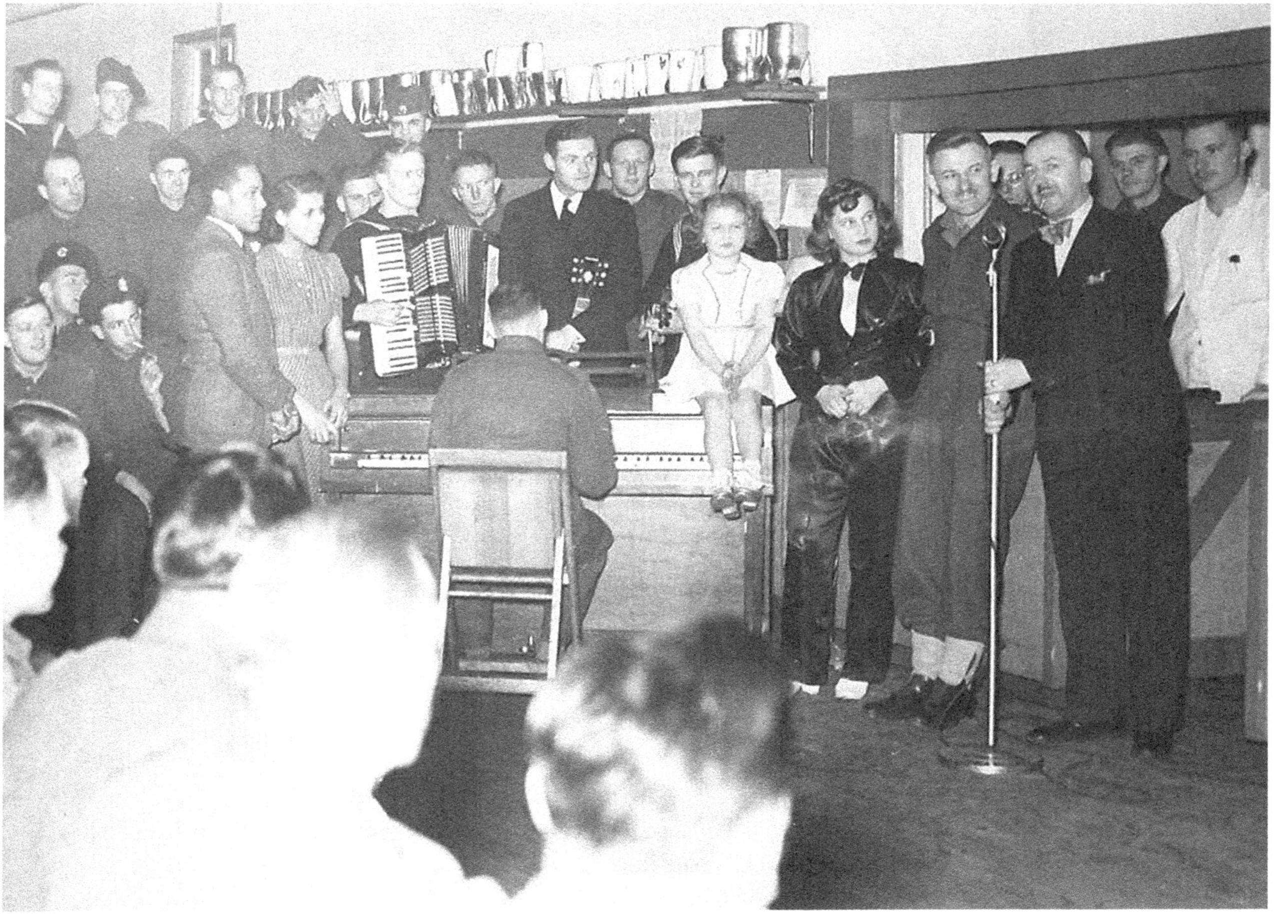

The White family including Portia and Lorne, the White Family Singers

me to the fact that numerous members of the white race, to which I belonged, seemed to look down on Negroes. In schoolyard games, we still sang "catch a nigger by the toe"; only later did a subsequent generation of children change it to tiger. I became aware that Negroes would not be welcome in the barbershops I visited; they had their own, in Negro areas. Restaurants too were for one race or the other. One of my younger sisters informs me that, after I left home and Africville was levelled, a petition attempting to prevent a couple of black families from moving to Kline Heights was circulated around the neighbourhood.

This was the period when a black woman was actually convicted of petty crime when her only transgression was sitting in the part of a New Glasgow movie theatre reserved for whites. When the absence of black workers in banks and other

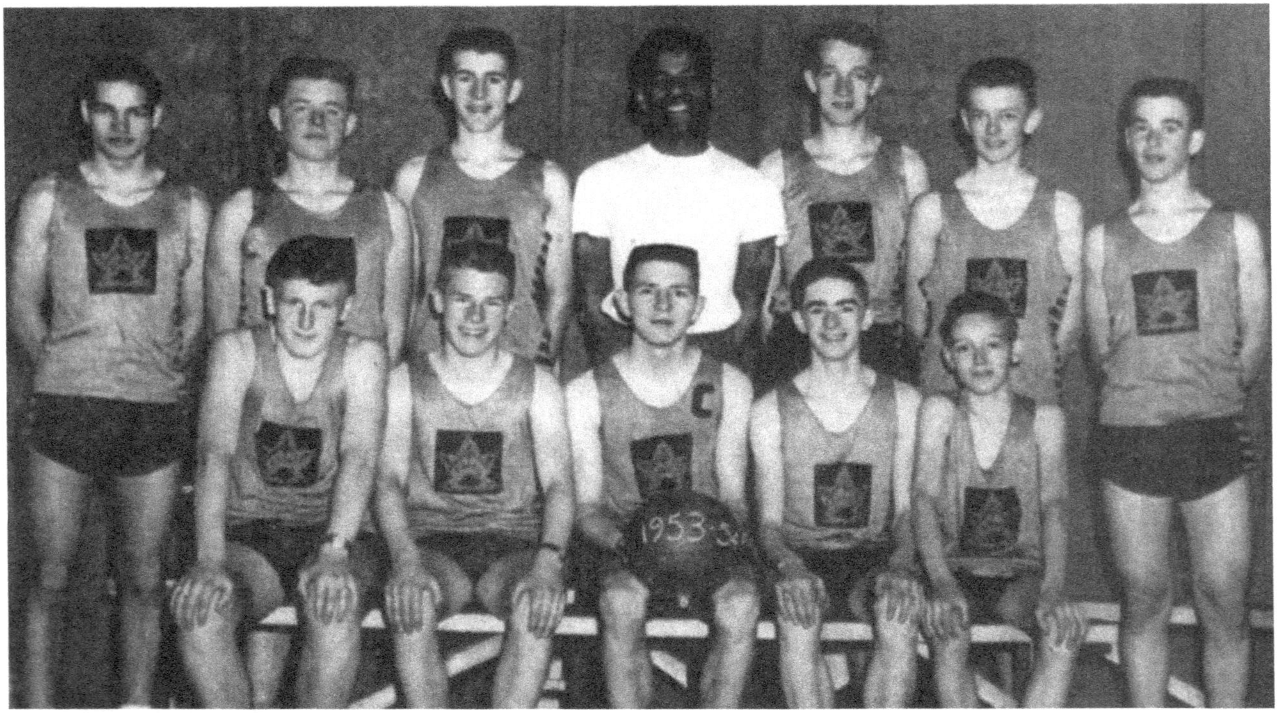

Senior basketball team, 1953 Armdale High

places of employment was noticed, someone was bound to offer the lame formula that has not entirely disappeared: Some white customers would not like having to deal with Negroes; it would be bad for business.

Of all racist aspects that were institutionalized in the society whose principles and practices I was learning to absorb, residential segregation was the most potent. Separate communities for blacks and whites meant that while schools in Halifax County were not officially segregated, black children attended small schools near their own homes, and there were no blacks in schools attended by whites. It wasn't until I entered the workforce at age seventeen that I finally encountered blacks daily at my elbow, in situations of shared concerns, joint activities and the possibility of friendship.

So, at that stage, was I some kind of a racist? I did not want to be. But I was very impressed, maybe somewhat blinded, by the idea of difference. I was in my late thirties before I formed such a close bond with one particular friend that, for the first time, I could be in the company of a black person for several hours before the thought came back that used to dominate my consciousness in such situations: He is black and I am white.

Given the institutionalized racism in Nova Scotia of the time, the hiring practices of the Armdale School Board are very interesting. The student body at South Armdale, where I attended, might have been one hundred per cent lily-white; nevertheless, we had some black teachers. The credit should perhaps go to the teachers. Were teachers in short supply, or did the School Board purposely give us black authority figures and role models to counteract the harmful outcomes of residential segregation?

In grades 6 and 7, we had Miss Barton, a black woman, as music teacher. She taught us "Squid Jiggin' Ground," which I thought at the time was a traditional old Newfoundland folk song. Only later did I learn it had been copyrighted by Art Scammell with sheet music produced only a few years earlier; this was a sign of how well she kept up with regional culture, white or black.

A few years later, Lorne White, youngest son of a famously talented black family, came to the school as teacher of physical education and basketball coach. Words can hardly describe how tremendously popular he was with all us white children. The boys all admired him because he was so athletic, funny and friendly. The girls loved him for more obvious reasons — so funny, friendly, handsome and sexy. Later he became a genuine celebrity, appearing as one of the regular performers on the TV show *Singalong Jubilee.*

That was forty years ago, but we still sometimes see reruns of old *Singalong* programs. When that happens, graduates of my days at Armdale High School draw near the TV. Their seventy-year-old voices become tinged with teenaged enthusiasm. You also hear notes of respect and affection, with no hint of the racism you might have expected, considering what mixed messages they received in their youth. They call out: "Look, it's Mr. White, he taught us gym."

CHAPTER 11 1942—49

Radio

Back in the 1940s, radio was the principal channel of popular culture. Then, radio carried everything, including a good deal of drama and general entertainment, and was often as strong a focus for family togetherness and shared experience as TV became later on. People would gather in the living room at scheduled times when certain programs came on. The radio was often a large, ornate, free-standing piece of wooden furniture that occupied a strategic area of floor space, with seating arranged around it. As their imaginations processed the dialogue and sound effects that came out of the fancy big box, listeners often found themselves (although it did not really help) staring at the radio. This was rehearsal, I suppose, for the television age soon to come.

People were attracted to the radio like iron filings to a magnet; what programs did they listen to back then? Digging into childhood memories, the programs I recall best were the ones with distinct signature openings that, through frequent repetition, embedded themselves in the brain for a lifetime.

For example, there was a family-oriented situation comedy featuring a boy in his early teens who got into various scrapes. Like all of our favourites, it came on at the same time each week. A suspenseful pause followed the close of the program before it, and then our show was announced by a woman's voice summoning her son, calling out in the usual maternal mixture of love and exasperation. He responded immediately, the answer wavering and high-pitched like a thirteen-year-old boy whose voice is beginning to crack and change.

Hen-ry! Henry Aldrich!
Coming, mother.

A crime drama with an equally memorable opening starred a superhero who — although you thought you knew where he was — could never be seen (this was radio after all).

Who knows what evil lurks in the hearts of men?
The Shadow knows [followed by a sinister laugh].
Heh, heh, heh, heh, heh.

Another opening segment that was not easily shaken from the head was from a popular quiz show from CBC Toronto. It had a live audience, but the gimmick was that people also wrote in from all over the country. Contestants coming up on stage picked an at-home partner by randomly plucking a letter out of a big drum. The partner would win (or not win) the same prizes as the person answering questions in front of the microphone. When the time arrived for this show to begin, the first sound was a whisper, increasing in volume with each of three repetitions. Then came the key word, repeated about six times, always louder. Finally, an excited shout: the name of the program.

Gold, silver, dollars.
Gold, silver, dollars.
Gold, silver, dollars.
Money money money money money money.

SHARE THE WEALTH! There are a couple of other presentations that I recall pretty clearly; they could be called service programs. One was Uncle Mel, who read and discussed the comics from the Halifax daily newspaper every day at 5 p.m.; this served two purposes. First, the strategic timing got the kids in from playing outside. I remember Mother calling me; I was glad to rush inside, spread the paper out on the floor and go over the comics with my radio uncle. Once that was finished, I found I had been cunningly trapped inside for supper. The program's other purpose, almost coincidental, was that we learned to read.

L for Lanky was also, I suppose, a service show — a wartime morale booster masquerading as an action drama. Lanky was a Lancaster bomber with a Canadian crew, flying from airfields in Britain to attack targets in Germany and occupied Europe. They had various crises and close calls, often flying back to the home base on one wing and a prayer.(This phrase comes from a wartime song lyric: "How we sang as we limped through the air.") People on the program usually experienced a happy ending — except for the enemy.

Radio featured many, and memorable, advertisements. The sponsor of the Joe Louis fights repeated their mantra frequently:

Gilette blue blades
With the sharpest edges ever honed.

My generation must have been the first in history to have known the meaning of "hone" from the age of five or six. Another famous formula from the era of radio ads boasted Ivory soap:

. . . ninety-nine and forty-four one-hundredths
per cent pure — it floats!

In many respects we were the typical radio-influenced family: awash in catchy commercials or dramatic slogans that resisted erasure from the mind; mesmerized by the electronic box; exposed to a continent-wide popular culture that ignored

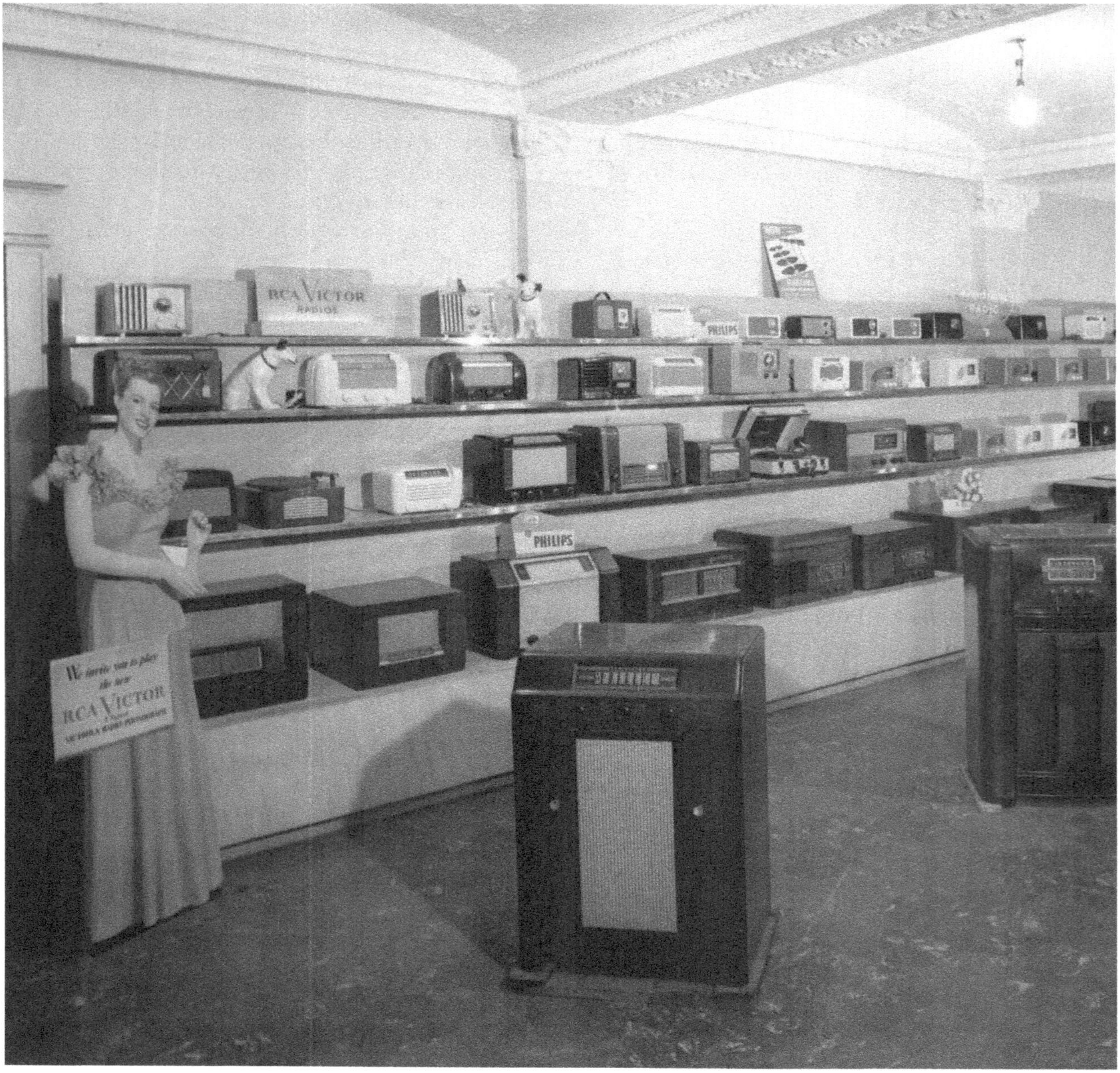

Phinneys on Barrington Street

international boundaries. But we were even more "radioized" than most families. Our father, long before he became Dad, was ham-operator of VE1GC.

Keeping his amateur radio station on the air was Dad's most persistent lifelong hobby. He loved nothing more than getting a metal box with the proper holes and openings to stuff and solder full of tubes, wires and general gadgetry until it became a transmitter-receiver. Then he went on the air with it, tweaked it into perfection, exchanged postcards with other ham operators he contacted — then disassembled it and built a new one, different in size, shape and range, though using some of the same parts.

When one of Dad's friends moved to Montreal, he let his local amateur's licence lapse. Years later, when he returned to Halifax, he went to amateur radio headquarters for reinstatement and was given a list of available call letters. Seeing VE1GC on the list was how he learned that Dad had died, for no lesser calamity could keep those dedicated amateurs off the air. His shocking realization was a very radio-like experience, for it was often the case with listeners that the key ideas they received came not via the medium, but their own imagination working with it.

CHAPTER 12 1950–52
Hoopville

In early twenty-first century, Halifax frequently hosted the university men's basketball championship tournament. The event generated huge crowds with a good deal of enthusiastic (sorry) hoop-la. Many people decided that the city had become one of Canada's principal basketball capitals. Some of us, however, knew that status had been achieved long before.

When I was a young teenager in Halifax in the early 1950s, the boys played basketball. Actually, there were some boys who played hockey, but basketballers tended to look down on them. Hockey players were burdened with a mountain of expensive gear that someone else probably paid for, and had to depend on grown-ups to drive them everywhere. By contrast, basketball players were much more independent. All we needed was a ball (someone in the group always had one), some free time not monopolized by parental planning, and sneakers, which we wore all the time anyway. Also, and this was the most challenging requirement, we needed a place to play.

As I recall, there were no outdoor courts in those days. There was no challenge during the weekdays. Catering to our basketball addiction, in a typical week, there would likely be a church league practice and game, a school game and practice, and several hours spent in someone's driveway trying out our latest style of jumpshot while parents worried about the windows. On Saturdays, though, we had to range about searching for an empty, enclosed space with a basket at each end.

Many school and church gyms were either locked up tight or going to waste (that is, dedicated to other activities). Denial of access to the incredibly spacious gymnasium at the naval base

HMCS *Stadacona* (STAD) — we heard it had glass backboards — was emphasized by the presence of armed sentries. Therefore, we had a big job to perform: to find a friendly hall rigged out in the proper fashion, unlocked, yet unoccupied.

Fortunately, we knew the location of all the church gyms — the Protestant ones. (For a while, we were not even sure whether Catholics played basketball.) So picture us on a Saturday afternoon, issuing from our neighbourhood in a group of three or four, perhaps linking up with another similar group as we walked along. And walked and walked, all over the city; but as I think I remember correctly, never failed to get a game going. Sometimes we finished up at St. Andrews church hall, upstairs on Coburg Road, the space later occupied by Nova Scotia College of Art before it scattered to its complicated locations all over historic properties and downtown. Sometimes we came to the cramped confines of United Memorial in the North End, to our own headquarters at Bethany United, or the tidy hall on Preston Street operated by the honourary Protestants of the Young Men's Hebrew Association.

Our ignorant uncertainty about Catholic basketball was settled on the occasion when Albert joined David and me in our Saturday search for a game. Albert had started his educational career at Father Martin's school (St. John the Baptist parish) in Melville Cove, before joining us at South Armdale. When his family moved in town, he attended St. Agnes Junior High, and later St. Mary's College, for high school. "Let's go down to St. Mary's," he said.

We argued a while before undertaking that long hike. At one time, St. Mary's had been very conveniently situated in the middle of town, where Quinpool Centre is now. A finely sculpted garden faced the crosstown street. In late afternoons, Jesuit fathers could be seen strolling there amid ornate shrubbery, reading or meditating. The college, however, had recently relocated to a bulldozed, treeless expanse at the south end of Robie Street.

We walked down Robie to the new St. Mary's. Sure enough, there was a fine gymnasium in the lower, rear extremities of the gigantic first building. Not only that, but it was the week between Christmas and New Year's and several boarders who had not been able to go home for the holidays were languidly lounging around. Energized by the appearance of new elements, they joined us, or we them. Soon a satisfying, fast-paced game with full complements of shirts and skins was underway.

Another memorable discovery was the Cogswell Street gym. It was located on the lower reaches of Citadel Hill, where Gottingen Street ends. Long forgotten now, the Cogswell gym was a military installation and already derelict and abandoned for several years before we blundered in there one drizzly Saturday. Who knows why it was unlocked that day? Maybe it was scheduled for a cleaning; if so, it was long overdue, with one-eighth of an inch of grime everywhere. All the dirt affected the game; we had to be cautious driving in for layups, having found that a decade's buildup of everything made the hardwood floor very slippery to land on. In all of our Saturday wanderings, this occasion was the only time a game had to be called short on account of dust.

CHAPTER 13 1952–61

Hitchhiking

A major characteristic of the 1940s and 1950s was how much more safe and secure people seemed to feel then, compared with recent years. One good example of this is the attitude towards hitchhiking. This method of travel has a bad reputation these days, after several well-publicized cases of crimes perpetuated against either hitchhikers or the drivers who picked them up and did not live to regret their kindness. My youth was a simpler, safer time. Both my parents encouraged their children in independent decision making and taking responsibility for themselves. As a result, I do not recall any opposition or discussion whatsoever when, from the age of fifteen, I began to disappear down various highways, whereabouts unknown, for whole days or part-weeks at a time.

During the next six years, I made twenty-one trips. I usually stayed within the Maritimes, often visiting my grandparents in Grand River, Cape Breton. The most ambitious journey, and my first overnight trip, was a nine-day late-summer excursion to Boston. Donald and I had both worked for the federal government for a year following Grade 12 and had a couple of weeks free before entering Dalhousie. We reached the St. Stephen, New Brunswick, border crossing into the United States just before suppertime the first day. Dusk found us in the heart of Maine. We stayed the night at a modest bed and breakfast in a small village strung out along the highway. Late the next afternoon, we arrived in Boston. My aunt and uncle and their two boys, younger than we were, gave us the royal treatment: an exploration of Harvard Square, a 3-D movie and — highlight — an afternoon game at Fenway Park. I saw Ted Williams! The journey home was another two days, with rides coming easily.

Hitchhiking

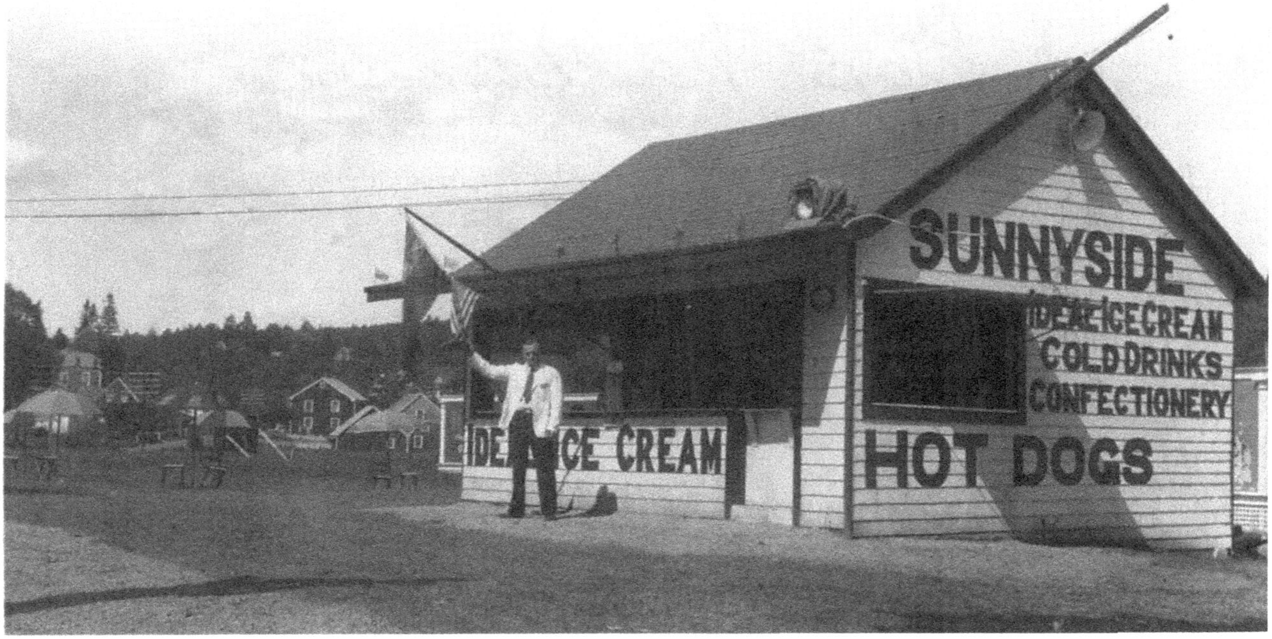

Sunnyside restaurant in Bedford, where most long-distance trips began

This was the first time I visited the United States; I noticed some differences. Rural homes and barns seen from the road were better maintained in the States than they were in the Maritimes; there were more paved roads; and the Americans had some yellow as well as white lines on their highways, a practice that had not yet started in our part of Canada. I was shocked, however, to see how basically similar New England was to Nova Scotia: family farms, prominent churches, corner stores with gas pumps and, especially, long stretches of countryside separating the very occasional small towns.

Although I was eighteen and allegedly well-informed, I apparently thought the United States would look very different from Canada. I think I somehow expected that as soon as we crossed the border, the scenery would immediately start resembling the background of action-hero comic books — urban not rural, crowded, dense and dangerous. Instead, it seemed as innocent and pastoral as home. Later, we saw Boston streetcars running into tunnels to become a subway, and that was more like the metropolis was supposed to be. My strongest overall impression, however, was one of sameness, not difference. Boston seemed to be nothing more than Halifax writ a little larger, and New England just a better-paved version of the Maritimes.

CHAPTER 14 1950—52

Boys' Parliament

A regional institution that had a decided impact on my youth was the Maritime Provinces Tuxis and Older Boys' Parliament. This was an annual meeting devoted to the discussion of serious affairs in a Christian atmosphere. It occurred over a three-day period between Christmas and New Year's at Mount Allison University, where residence facilities had been vacated for the holidays and were available to accommodate the boy parliamentarians.

This unique gathering was the cooperative climax and capstone of the religious education effort in a range of Protestant churches. Each congregation in the United Church, the Church of Christ and various Baptist, Pentecostal and other denominations had the right to send a couple of boys, most of whom eventually became ministers of religion. Roman Catholics did not participate.

"Tuxis" was a word heard around the United Church at that time. It was a program of church-centred activities for boys aged sixteen to eighteen, following on from Trail Rangers, which catered to ages thirteen to fifteen. These programs were somewhat similar to the more familiar Wolf Cubs and Boy Scouts youth groups. Cubs and Scouts, however, had secular concerns and were devoted to good citizenship and self-reliance ("Be prepared"); while the Trail Ranger and Tuxis path promoted spiritual and religious values. We repeated our official goal in words taken directly from the Bible: "And Jesus increased in wisdom and stature/And in favour with God and man."

I was initially tagged to attend the regional Tuxis parliament by the minister of our church. The first time I attended, at age fourteen, I was a couple of years younger than most of that year's first-time members. See me therefore, two days

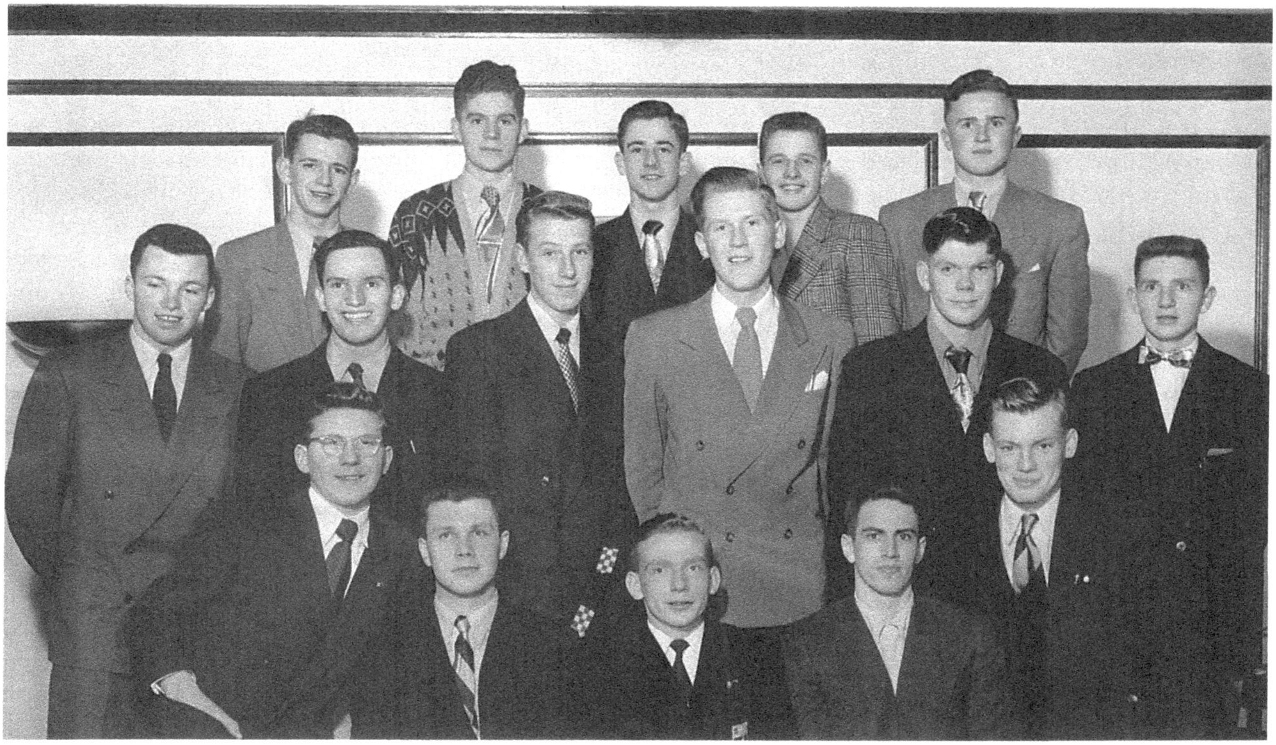

Government at Older Boys' Parliament 1953 (author in bow tie)

after Christmas, leaving the house with Dad in the early morning. We walked down to the corner of Quinpool and Chebucto to catch the trolley. Dad carried my little suitcase. It was very cold, well below 32 degrees Fahrenheit. (We were still using the old thermometer.) The snow-covered ground recorded our every footstep with a crunchy sound.

The Number 5 trolley deposited us at the train station attached to the old Nova Scotian Hotel. Dad made sure I had my ticket and that I got on the correct train. Then he went to work and left me alone. As I was leaving home for a several-day visit among strangers with no family members, I was quietly crying as the train pulled out of the station. There were other boys on board, bound for the same destination as me; after stops at Rockingham and Bedford, there were more of them. Long before we reached Waverley, I was talking and laughing with these new friends and had entirely forgotten about being homesick.

Parliamentarians disembarked just across the provincial border in Sackville, New Brunswick. We were met by one of the organizers, with transportation provided to take us to the Mount Allison campus. For the duration of Parliament, home would be Trueman House, a new, rather fancy residence with a grand entryway. We were assigned rooms, and if the regular occupants had left any of their gear unstowed, we were told not to disturb it. My roommate and I, however, were leafing through a pile of magazines when we came across one that featured shapely women much too scantily dressed for midwinter. Although it was then still the pre-*Playboy* era, these girls had lost most of their clothing with no help from Hugh Hefner. While we were ogling the results, in came an older boy, scolding and reproving — remember we were a very religious, conservative lot. He ordered us to leave the dirty pictures alone. As I recall, we did so (except for maybe one last peek just before leaving for home).

Regular sessions of Parliament were a great training in public speaking, and in the decorum of conducting meetings. "I beg leave to give notice that at the next session of this house, I will move, seconded by Mr. Smith, that ..." Generally, everyone agreed on the main subjects discussed — the regulation of alcohol (other drugs had not yet become a problem), the benefits of immigration and the need for social justice as well as individual regeneration. There was sufficient disagreement about the details, however, that the parliamentary approach was appropriate. After an election, one group formed the government, with ministers bringing forward various resolutions. They were faced, on the other side of the long clerk's table that divided the room, by a smaller group, the loyal opposition, who opposed and debated against the government's proposals.

The meetings were full of ritual. A mace was carried in and out to signify the start and end of business. Prayer preceded everything. An older boy, well experienced as a former Premier, presided as Speaker. He wore a black academic gown and mortarboard cap. Whenever he had something to say, he rose from his seat — this was the signal for everyone else to stop talking — and doffed the cap. Two or three younger boys from the local area had been well trained to act as parliamentary pages. They sat on both sides of the Speaker and rose or sat when he did, unless they were carrying notes from one member of parliament to another, bringing glasses of water or fetching requested documents from the central table. Even during my first attendance at Parliament, I worked up enough nerve to make a few interjections in the debate, or pose questions to a minister. The greatest orator I remember was one of the Ihasz boys from Sydney, who began a speech with this admission, shocking to me: "I am a D.P." (In 1950, anti-immigration politics often accused Displaced Persons from Europe of taking jobs away from home-born Canadians.)

On our last night in Sackville, a very impressive watchnight service was held. Here again, the stagecraft was impeccable. This religious service started at a hitherto-unheard of time: 11 p.m. It was held in the upstairs chapel of a university building. The organ music was muted and slow; even our singing was whispered. The leader who spoke urged us to know Jesus as a personal saviour, as he seemed to. He called us to dedicate our pure young lives to God's service. Closing, he asked us to return to our rooms soberly, with no chatter, go right to bed, and think about the opportunities opening before us.

Parliament led me to be more spiritual. It also made me more ambitious to lead and to represent. After attending two years, I put myself forward as a candidate to be elected president of our high school students' union. My opponent was more popular with members of our peer-group of grade 10 and 11 student but I focused on younger students. I won, by a very narrow margin.

CHAPTER 15 1953—54

Queens and Kings for a Year — Grade 12

In the years right after World War II, educational arrangements on the outskirts of Halifax were in a state of flux. It still remained the case that the only fully developed high school programs were in Halifax itself. Out in the county, neighbourhood schools reached right through the elementary years up to Grade 11. Then school planners got a little more ambitious. One result, when we were in Grade 7 at South Armdale, was a construction project right in our schoolyard.

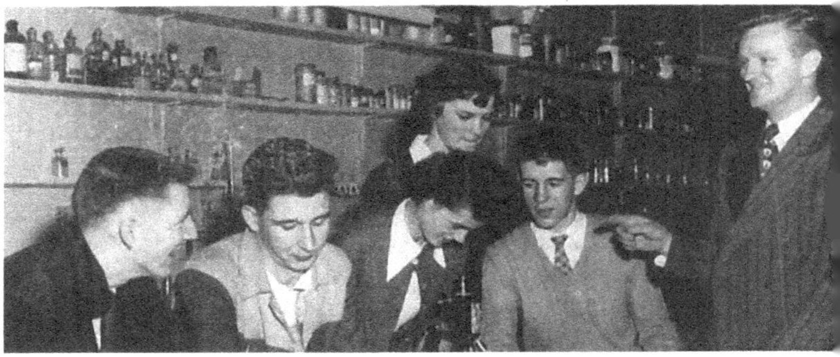

Armdale High School biology lab

The new building that resulted, of shiny white stucco, was Armdale High — an institution distinct from South Armdale primary/elementary (big, boxy, wooden, ugly brown) with which it shared a schoolyard. At first, the high school accommodated grades 7 to 11. After a while, Grade 12 was added. The first time it was offered, there were three pupils.

The following year, in the fall of 1953, I became part of a Grade 12 class that was, once again, very small. Bill, Dave, Joan, Kay, Mac and Phil constituted the full complement of clients at that senior level. Since students from Fairview and North Armdale transferred in to swell the population, Armdale High had two Grade 10s and two Grade 11s — but

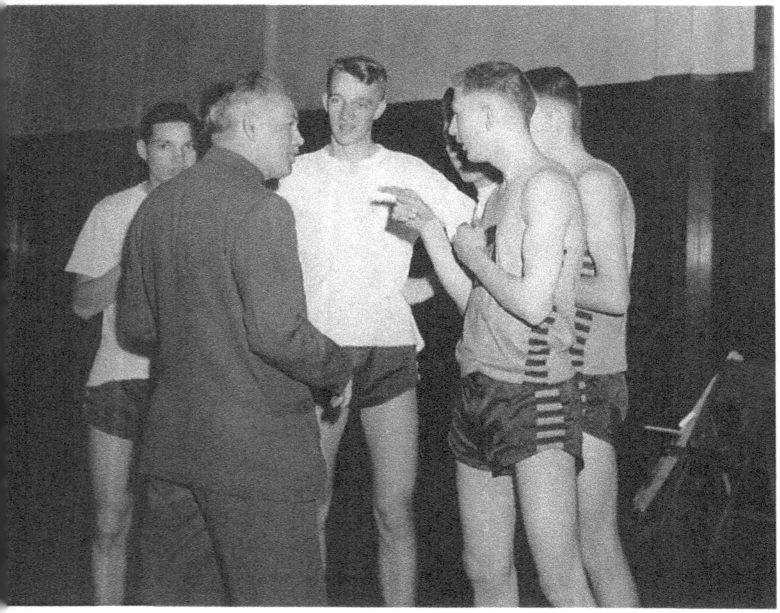

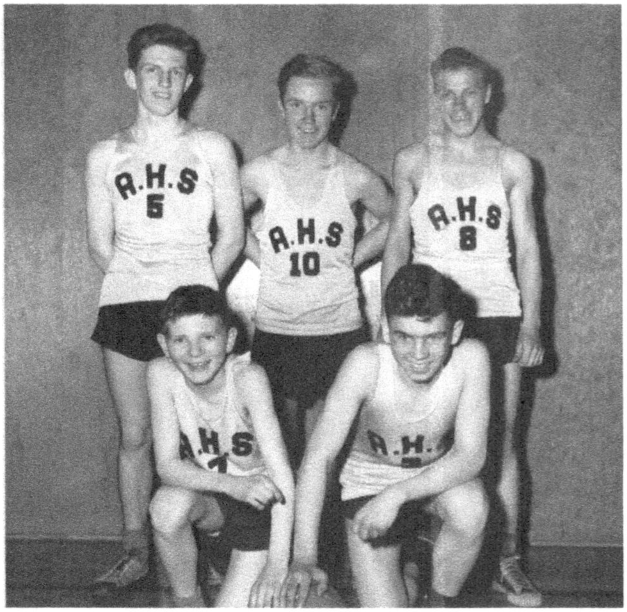

Left: Who's telling who? Author with Principal Carl Purdy
Right: Armdale High School basketball team

almost nobody in Grade 12. Why were there so few?

The answer seems threefold. At that time, Grade 11 (junior matriculation) was widely seen as the completion of high school. Grade 12 courses were in a different category: eligible for university credit. Secondly, in many families, there was an established custom for Grade 12 students to attend city schools. The habit persisted even when Grade 12 became available closer to home. And there was no doubt a suspicion that the standard of instruction at upstart Armdale High would be inferior to that at city schools, with their more solid tradition in senior matriculation studies. So, there were only six of us, four boys and two girls.

Looking back over a lifetime of instructional situations in various classrooms, the most pleasurable and rewarding of all those academic terms was the year I spent in Grade 12 at Armdale High School. Think of the special situation we were in, the only seventeen-year-olds in a school populated on one side by 150 bustling, childish thirteen- to sixteen-year-olds, and at the other extreme by eight or nine subject teachers, headed by the principal with his public address system. We were the in-between group — us, dignified senior students, unharried by the regulations and herding that were forced upon the mob, unhurried by the worries and duties that beset our busy teachers. In a group so small, discipline problems never arose. Except for the important stipulation that we be in certain classrooms at certain times, we were left pretty much alone and trusted to come and go as we pleased: honourary faculty members, almost.

CHAPTER 16 1955

Armdale Rotary

An earlier episode explained the many-sided importance, to Armdale-ites living in the county, of the five-way intersection at the head of the Northwest Arm. We went there for shopping, public transit, post office and numerous other amenities. During the good weather season of 1955, we acquired another reason to be goin' down the Arm. It was to watch the progress of construction on the Armdale Rotary.

Knots of onlookers, sidewalk superintendents, would gather from time to time on the avenues leading into the construction area. They debated the merits and hazards of what was being produced under that permanent cloud of dust and exhaust fumes. Factions developed.

We teenagers were at first opposed to the rotary, because it swallowed our softball field. The actual Armdale circle, when it emerged, occupied the same space where the outfield used to be, with home plate somewhat uphill near the fringe of trees around St. James Anglican Church. Most of us came around, however, to admire the rotary's slick, efficient appearance: clean, curved lines, fresh new curbs and pristine paving. Many of us thought it the latest word in modern and — the highest accolade we ever bestowed — just like the States.

Many adult onlookers agreed with our final approval. Others, however, disagreed with the rotary's basic premise — that steady streams of traffic could cross without vehicles ever having to stop; stop-and-go lights eliminated in a perpetual motion arrangement. They predicted that uncertainty in drivers would produce a holocaust of crashes in the circle, and rush-hour snarls that would back vehicles up for miles on all five of the approach

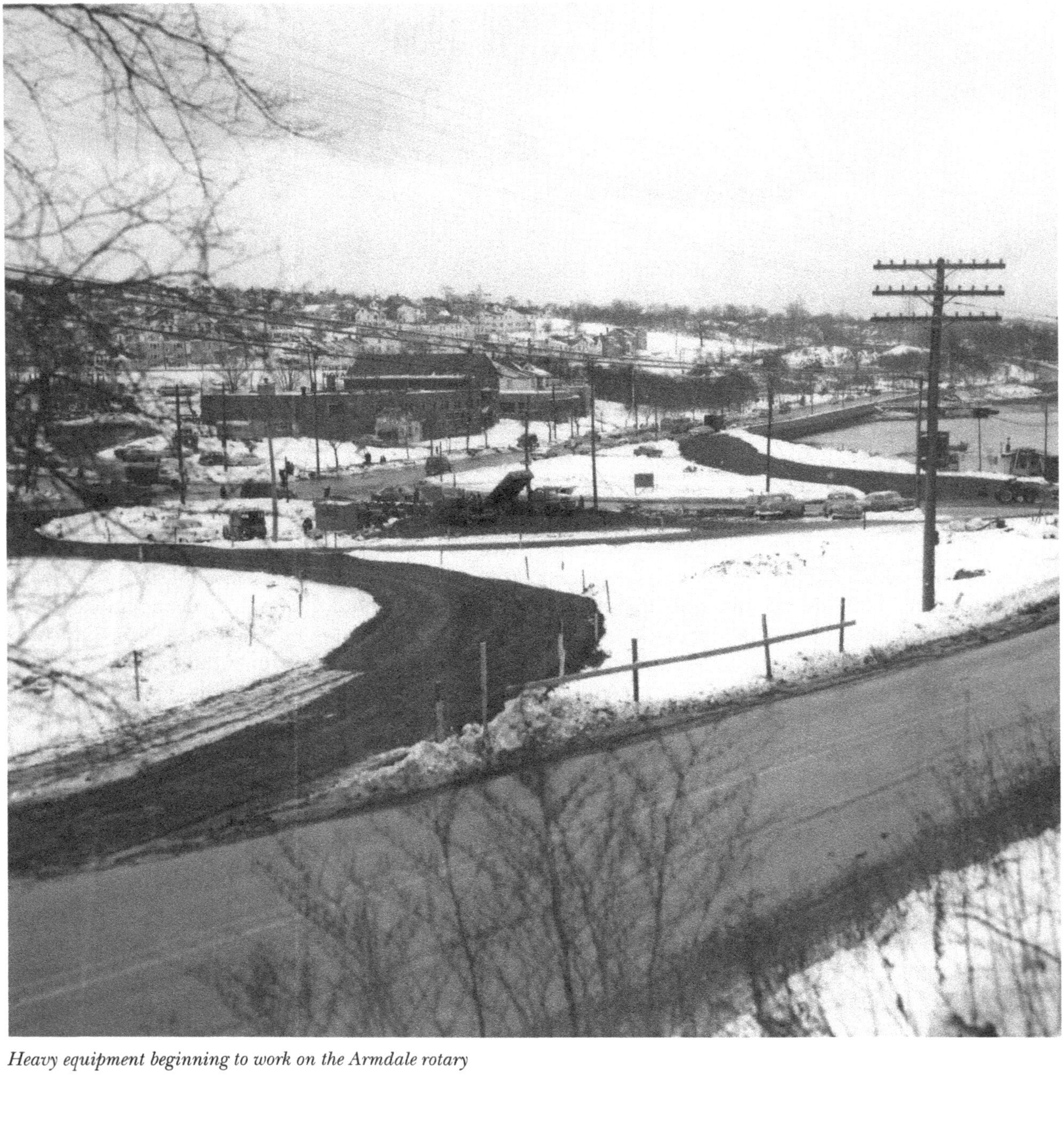

Heavy equipment beginning to work on the Armdale rotary

roads. It was among these rotary deniers that the urban legend was launched about the car trapped on the Armdale circle for hours on end, maybe forever, unable to exit. Their best advice for motorists: Better keep a good supply of sandwiches and drinking water in the vehicle, just in case.

The realignment of roads and evenly spaced entrances to the inner circle gradually emerged as work went forward. One scenic highlight was the transport of a huge boulder, seven or eight feet in diameter. When I passed by one day, it was resting in the back of a dump truck that was pointed towards Herring Cove Road. When I came by again an hour later, the boulder had apparently shifted. The back end of the truck was now weighed right down to the ground, while its front wheels idled helplessly six feet in the air. While I was enjoying the moment's amusement ... Hey, just a minute! I recognized this boulder. The top half of it previously decorated our softball field, poking out of the ground near second base. Any ball bouncing off it might fly erratically in any direction, so we decided any such occurrence would be considered a ground rule double.

Who now recalls that the building housing the front part of today's Armview Restaurant and Lounge began life as the Armview Grill, on the other side of the rotary? Part of the rotary project was clearing away what little development there was at the head of the Northwest Arm. Other buildings were simply demolished, but the Grill was worth trying to save.

"Trying" is the operative word. Moving that large, square building was in fact the trickiest aspect of the whole rotary construction project. It was tall enough that all overhead wires had to be taken down and alternative arrangements made for continued electrical and telephone service (no cable or internet in those days) in that part of town. The Grill's original location was at the exact head of the Arm, with salt water lapping the back doorstep. It took two nights and a day to move the building from its original site, one-quarter of the way around the rotary in progress and a short distance up Chebucto Road, where it was eased onto its new foundation.

People in the committees of onlookers were making bets just where along that route the building would be dropped to the ground or shaken into pieces. They all lost their wagers. Nevertheless, when the renovations that promoted the old Grill into today's Restaurant/Lounge were undertaken, the carpenters came with a question. They wanted to know if the building had been through an earthquake. While it was not obvious to the naked eye, carpenters' instruments revealed there was no perfectly level floor in the whole building.

CHAPTER 17 1943–52

Books

With help from family and teachers, Uncle Mel taught me to read, over the radio, when I was six years old. Reading quickly became a very favourite pastime. How favoured it was is signalled to me by two remembered circumstances.

For one thing, on every boyhood Christmas for a number of years, the present I appreciated most — ahead of skates or sleds, mitts or model airplanes — was books. On Christmas morning, if there were several books in my stash of loot, I would arrange them in a pile with the most preferred items on top. Through the afternoon, while neighbourhood friends might be clamouring to go out to dive through snowdrifts, careen down hillsides, that sort of thing, I would be quietly squirrelled away in a corner somewhere, working my way down through the pile of preferences.

The other early sign that I was hooked on reading was my patronage of the classroom libraries for grades 1 to 8 in the little school that I attended. Chapter 3, Cunard School, explained how by the end of Grade 4, I had read almost all the books available in that little school. Fortunately, we moved houses that summer and I started at a much larger school, with a new and expanded set of reading possibilities.

What did I read? The simple answer is almost everything. After the *Run, Spot, Run* variety of simple stories that there must have been, I encountered more complicated shenanigans in books about the Bobbsey twins, and the series of *Tom Swift* books, actually two Toms, father and son, both inventors. Quite early, as well, I recall an American fighter pilot, *Dave Dawson on Guadalcanal.* Aerial combat was the exciting part; I

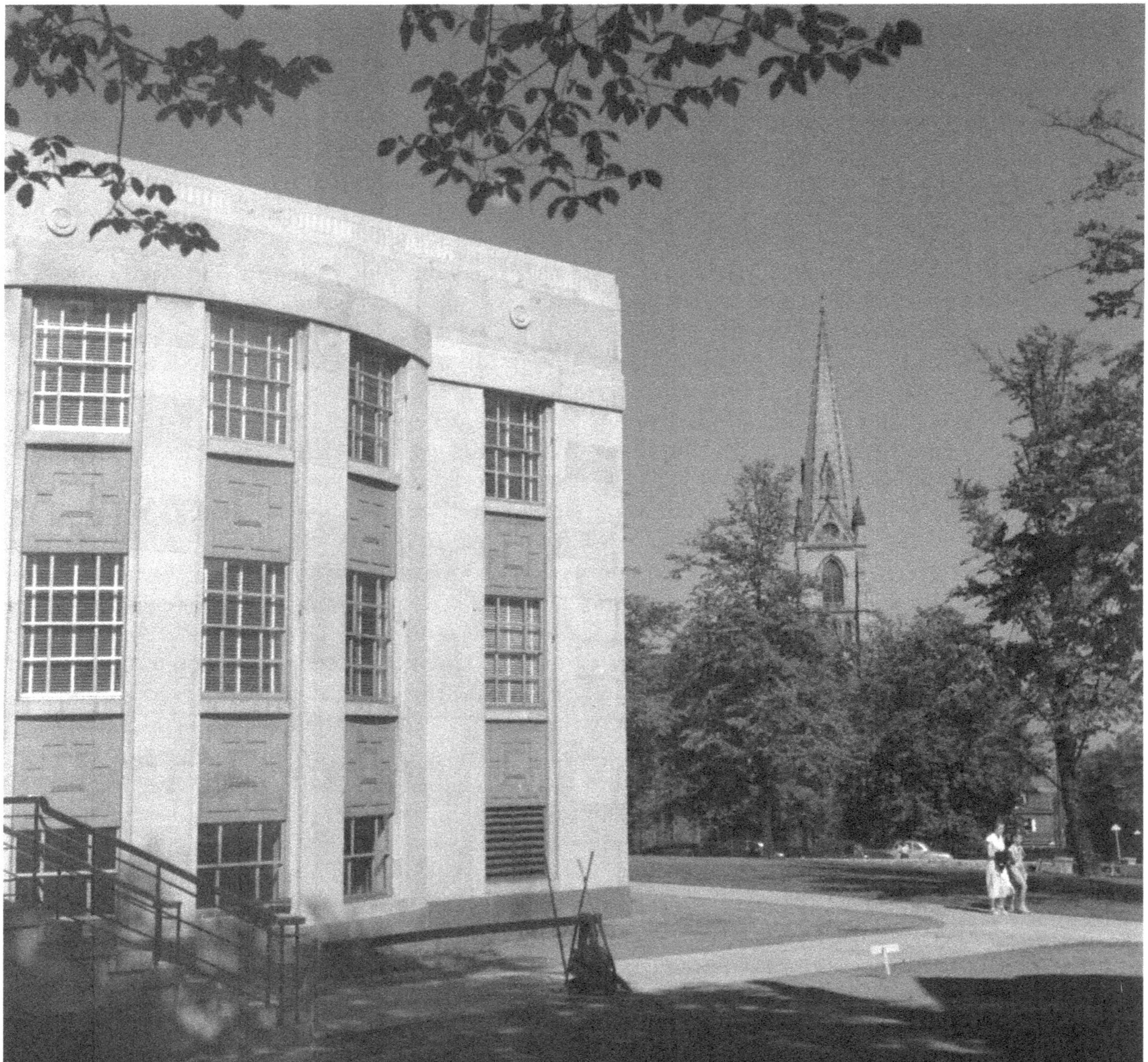

Halifax Memorial Library when new

had no interest in looking up where Guadalcanal might be located, only ruminating, offhandedly, that it was rather confusing if what seemed to be named as a waterway also masqueraded as an island.

What did I read? The simple answer — everything — is somewhat misleading, for I was always, you might say, a discriminating reader. For one thing, in the first several reading years, I am sure I leaned mostly on fiction. The half of available literature that dealt with the real world was outside my sphere of interest. Then a few cunning authors began sneaking in factual information that eventually whetted one's appetite and altered preferences, until by teenage times, I was reading mostly non-fiction: biographies and history.

After stabilizing for a while in the genre of war adventures, around age ten my interest shifted to a new category of fiction: animal stories. One book that comes to mind is *Buff, a Collie,* by Albert Payson Terhune. For the first time, now, I recall the name of that particular author, perhaps because I had just changed neighbourhoods and schools, and my new best friend was also named Albert. In this genre, there was also a voluminous set of books by Thornton W. Burgess. He wrote about *Old Mother West Wind* and her various animal friends — squirrels, chipmunks, foxes, weasels — with a book, or more than one, devoted to each personality.

The first serious non-fiction I recall — entirely voluntary, not triggered by suggestions or demands of home or school — was Winston Churchill's six-volume history of the Second World War. The series began to appear in 1948, with publication dates at annual intervals for the next few years. I caught up with most of these books soon after they became available. In a way, this was a continuation and intensification of the British education that I was receiving anyway in Armdale schools. On the other hand, Churchill's discussion of episodes and phases in the Battle of the Atlantic kept bringing to my attention the strategic significance of the place where I happened to live. Halifax, and the cargoes and navies that issued from the port, took on a foggy lustre not previously possessed. For me, therefore, the great leader's account of the world-wide struggle came with a hint about the possible importance of local and Canadian affairs.

Access to Terhune, Churchill and all the other literature in which I was interested became much easier after the Halifax Memorial Library opened in 1951 (when I was fourteen). If Halifax had a public library before this time, Mother — and by extension the rest of us — did not patronize it. Instead, Mother used the services of a lending library the Timothy Eaton Company operated on the second floor of its big downtown department store. There may have been a slight charge for books borrowed at Eaton's, or perhaps it was the case of a good corporate citizen stepping up to fill a void in a way that also brought customers into the store. At any rate, the new library on Spring Garden Road, a free service with a much larger collection than Eaton's, quickly became a major destination for family trips into town.

I developed a special and personal relationship with the library the following summer. Dad had arranged a summer job for me at the Maritime Telegraph and Telephone Company building on Sackville Street near the library. On-duty hours were devoted to helping lubricate and maintain telephone equipment, but for an hour at noon-time, I was free. The routine I adopted was to bolt down the sandwich I had brought from home, then stroll over to the library to read.

The best book I discovered that summer was

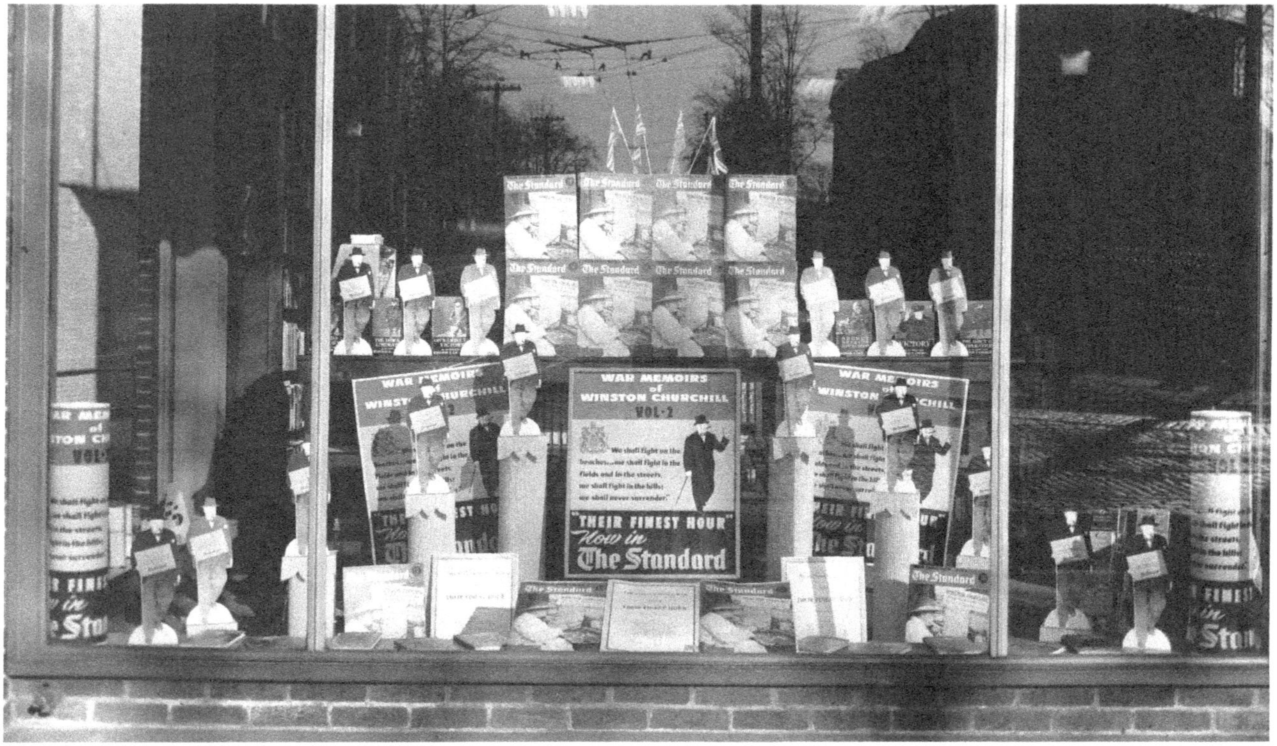

Complete set of Churchill's books on World War II

the recently published *Pitcairn's Island.* Last item in a trilogy, it described the aftermath of the famous mutiny on the British warship *Bounty* in the late 1700s. After setting Captain Bligh and his loyalists adrift in an open boat, the mutineers returned to Tahiti. Taking on board a community of girlfriends and hangers-on, they sailed away to a hideout on an uninhabited, uncharted island in the South Pacific. Their settlement on Pitcairn's became permanent when one faction, fearing British naval justice anywhere else, reduced the temptation to leave by burning the *Bounty.* None of the mutineers was ever brought to trial, and their descendants thrived well enough on their lonely outpost island through to the 1900s.

I found it fascinating reading, and made my way through it that August twenty minutes at a time. Instead of borrowing the book and having to carry it around, however, I decided to check and see if what they say is true, that the best place to hide a book is in a library. After my first session with *Pitcairn's Island,* I did not put the book back on its proper shelf. I was afraid that someone interested in British navy and South Sea Islands might see it there and borrow it out from under me. Instead, when no librarian was looking, I squirrelled it away in a shadowy corner devoted to very alien subjects: physics and biology if I remember correctly. It worked. Through the closing weeks of my first summer as a telephone boy, I read the whole account of the Pitcairn pioneers without any awkward interruptions.

All my life, ever since Uncle Mel first demonstrated the code for deciphering the utterances of comic-strip cats and cartoon crooks, I have been walking into libraries looking for something to read. The right books have made themselves very evident. It sometimes happens that in a back, darkened corner of a newly discovered library, shadows are restlessly leaping and dancing, as if the *Bounty* mutineers were still burning the big ship that took them to their paradisal hideaway/prison. On shelves here and there, a few of the items, eventually including a due proportion of girls' books, also draw attention to themselves. They practically slide back and forth in their allotted little spaces, or tilt up their spines so titles and call numbers can be more easily read. If the library is very quiet, you can almost hear them speak. In low voices courteously insistent and hugely promising, they say: "Read me, read me."

CHAPTER 18 1954—55

Pier 21 — Detention Quarters

I first entered the full-time workforce after completing Grade 12. A couple of friends had the same plan I did: to work for a year and get some money saved before enrolling in university. The best bet for employment seemed to be the federal government. We all three wrote the public service examination for general clerical duties, passed and received offers. It was like a lottery. One of us went to an office in the naval dockyard, issuing supplies to ships. One became a file clerk in a giant bureaucracy, either National Health and Welfare or Unemployment Insurance Commission. And I was offered the position of clerk-cashier in the catering office at the Department of Citizenship and Immigration.

The reason my outcome was luckier than my chums was not because the work was more challenging or more interesting. In fact, much of the work I did during my fourteen months at Immigration was repetitive, unskilled and downright menial. Where I lucked out was in my job's location. Pier 21 is where I was sent to work.

In the southern reaches of Halifax, behind the new railway station, which replaced the one destroyed in the 1917 explosion, Ocean Terminals has the deepest-water berths in the whole harbour. Ships of all sizes, up to the world's largest, tie up alongside at a wharf that runs along harbourside for a full mile. The seawall of this wharf is flanked by an apron of generous width, on the landward side of which there is a substantial, two-storey shed running the full length. Pier 21 is the middle portion of this building.

Landward again, when I worked there, lay a rail line that has since been decommissioned. On the city side of the rail line was a tall, single-storey shed

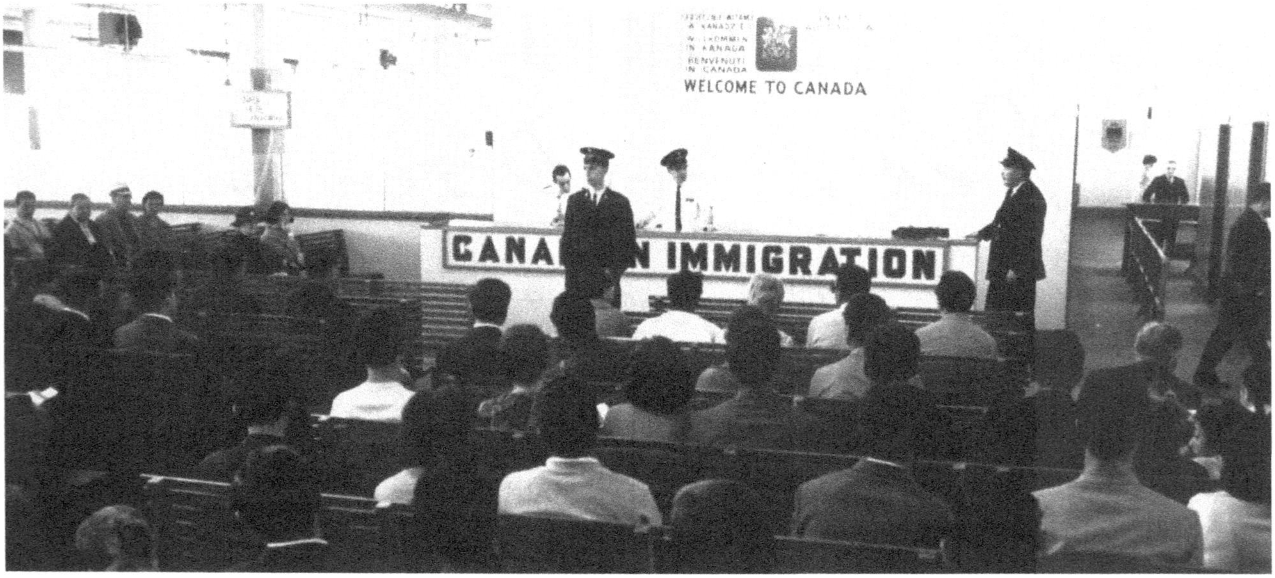

[Immigration Shed]

known as the immigration annex. Coming to work, Immigration employees — inspectors, guards, managers, clerical and kitchen staff — would mount a set of stairs attached to the annex and cross over the tracks by skywalk. My usual office was on Pier 21's second storey. I had a window that looked out to the harbour, viewing any ships that happened to be berthed there and those arriving from everywhere in the world, with picturesque Georges Island in mid-stream. I was clerk-cashier, but I actually had a second workstation. The other was at the canteen in the annex.

One reason why Immigration needed a catering department was to feed the inhabitants of detention quarters. A sort of gentle jail occupied part of the space at Pier 21. At any time that winter, there were from as few as a dozen to over a hundred persons being accommodated (held, confined) in detention there. It was because their papers were not quite in order, or they were waiting for additional cash, certificates or affidavits to arrive, or unfortunately, they had been ordered deported and were awaiting transport.

The catering department operated a cafeteria that served three meals a day to detainees. Since we were in the restaurant business anyway, noontime offerings were expanded to serve meals to Immigration employees and anyone else who happened to be looking for lunch along that part of the waterfront. At one end of the cafeteria was a well-equipped kitchen with the usual ovens, and cold and normal storage; at the other end, a door led into my workstation, which was an anteroom leading to offices occupied by the director and assistant director of catering. At the kitchen end, the staff consisted of two cooks and two or three servers and washers-up, plus a squad of casual

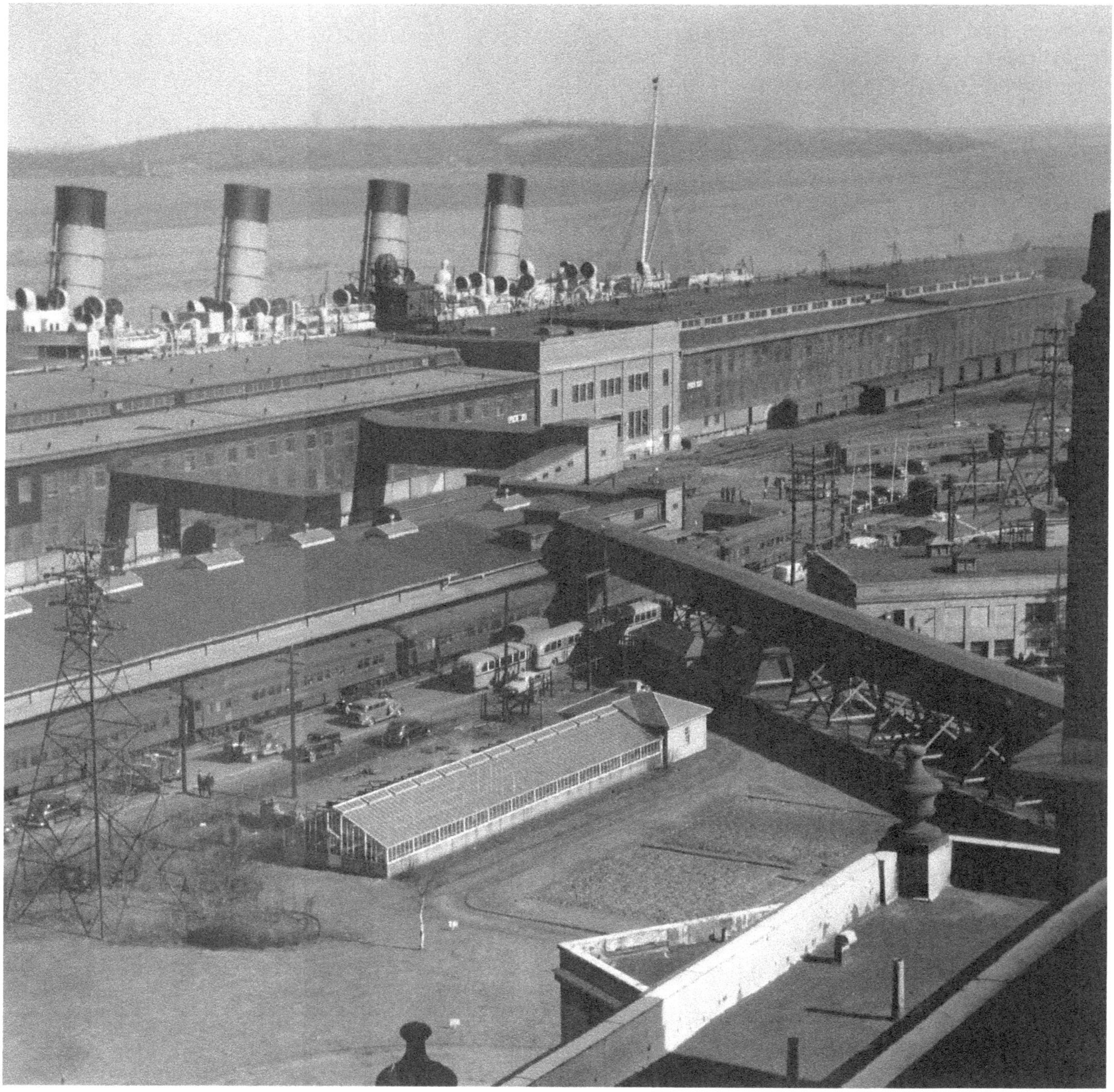

Overhead walkway linking the Immigration Annex to Pier 21

workers that expanded or contracted according to the number of folk in detention.

In the dining hall part of my job, I did not have a whole lot to do. I assisted with ordering supplies while the cooks handled all of the receiving and storing. There was cash to be counted, coins rolled and trips to the closest bank (at Hollis and Morris streets). I kept timesheets on employees. I typed up simple menus for the cafeteria choices, which were always so simple they were easily abbreviated: Mondays, fried pot; Tuesdays, mashed pot; Wednesdays, steamed pot; and so on.

Although the Immigration cafeteria was located right in detention quarters, I did not get to know many of the detainees. Most of them were there for only a short time, and there was usually a language barrier. One group I did get to know well was a family from England, consisting of the mother and two teenagers. The oldest child, a girl about my own age, had permission to travel around Halifax (some of us called this "going ashore"). She went out daily, seeking employment, and soon was hired onto the clerical staff at Ben's Bakery. When she began working there, the family became landed immigrants and moved into their own accommodation ashore; perhaps the lack of a steady income was all that had been keeping them in detention. I stayed in touch with these new Canadians for some time, on account of the girl.

CHAPTER 19 1954—55

Pier 21 – Boat Days

During the fourteen months I worked in the catering department at Canada's most famous immigration location, our second function was to operate a small grocery store for the benefit of newly arriving immigrants.

The store — we called it "canteen" — was located at one end of the hollow, echoing immigration annex. "Boat days," when migrants would arrive in groups of several hundred at a time, occurred once or twice a week. The usual routine saw them coming off their ship in the morning and early afternoon. Then came several hours of interviews, examination and processing by the Immigration inspectors.

The inspectors were the demigods of the Pier 21 operation. Unlike everyone else, they understood the complicated Immigration Act and its voluminous, finely-honed regulations. They decided who could properly be admitted to Canada, who had to go back, and who must be detained. Meanwhile, as inspectors examined the day's batch of immigrants, over in the annex the catering department was furiously stocking shelves and making sandwiches.

On the shelves in our canteen were the simplest of foodstuffs: bread, canned meat and fruit, soft drinks, cookies, crackers and spreads. Our sandwiches were usually cheese or ham, or sometimes, when a fit of creativity struck the boss, ham and cheese. Making these sandwiches was a marvel of efficiency. The two managers, myself and three or four casual workers brought in for boat day worked at it together. Slices from two or three loaves of bread at a time were spread on a large surface. We buttered each slice, cost-effectively, by melting the butter first and applying it very sparingly with a brush.

In an assembly-line operation, someone slapped on the ingredient, someone else the second slice,

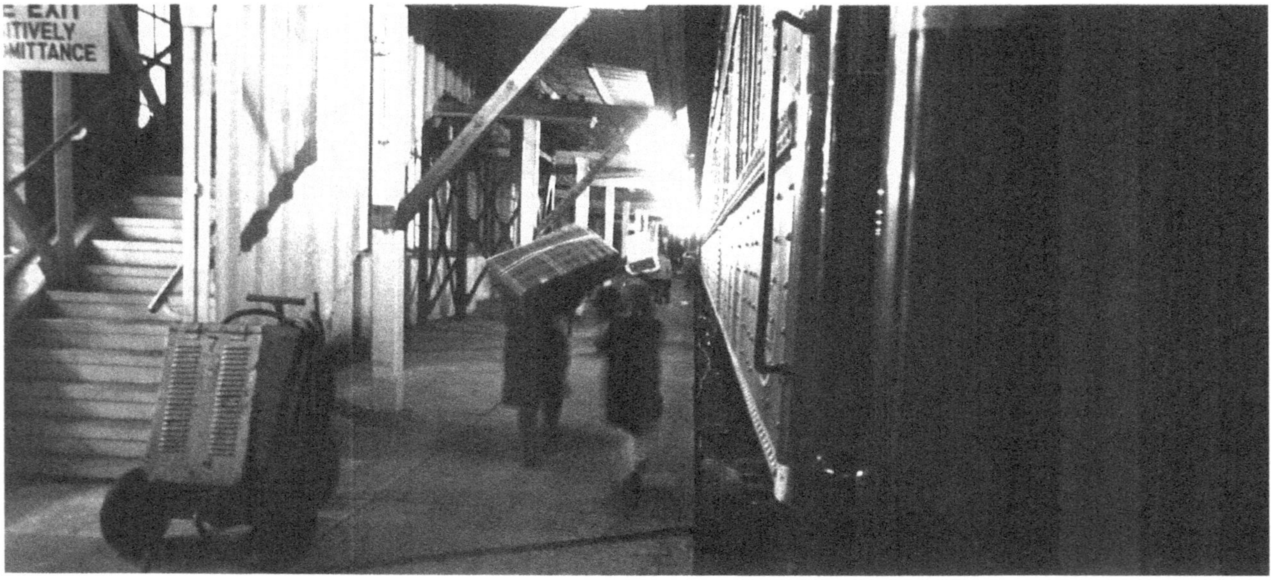

CN train waiting for passengers outside the immigration annex

someone cut the result into two pieces and someone wrapped it. Just once there was a bad delay. To cut each sandwich in two, one of the casual workers would draw a knife across it, while pressing down on the blade's dull edge with her other hand. On this occasion, in a rush, she accidentally had the knife's sharp edge pointing upwards. She was able to stop before doing herself permanent damage, but there was a lot of blood. The rumour that our cost-conscious boss sold the nearby sandwiches as strawberry something is grossly exaggerated.

The rationale behind our grocery store operation, often explained to me although I never saw it committed to paper (and perhaps it could not be) was this: Once processed and admitted to Canada, almost all the immigrants were destined to go forward to Montreal on special trains that CN operated for the purpose. They would need to eat on the twenty-four-hour journey, but once on board the train, they would be captive customers for high prices. Inspectors therefore advised the immigrants, while they waited in the annex, to stock up on food supplies at our non-profit, low-cost canteen.

They began flooding into the annex in the late afternoon to wait for trains that left at nine, ten, eleven or midnight. Now we made up for any indolence in the other half of the catering operation by becoming extremely busy. Customers stayed in single file as they entered the canteen from the queue outside and passed along our narrow aisle choosing items that they usually carried in baskets, rather than carts, to save space. They ended the tour at my cash register, where I took payment. Meanwhile, others were selling hot and cold beverages and sandwiches for the trip through a window that opened to the waiting area from the far end of the canteen.

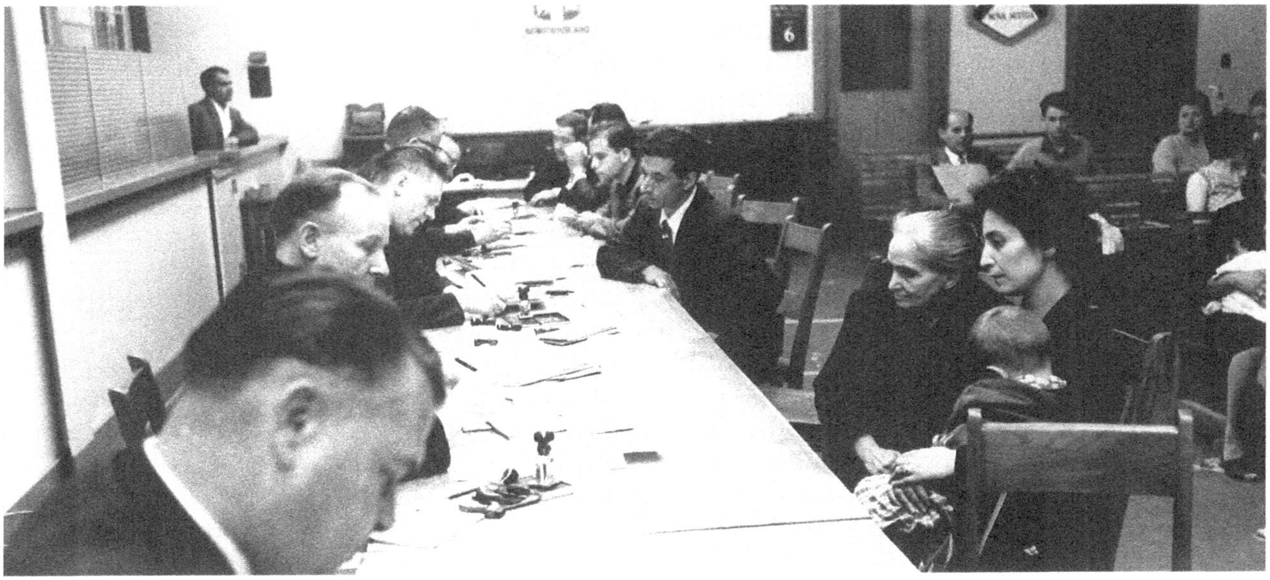

Recent immigrants being interviewed by Canadian inspectors.

Many families came through the grocery lineup more than once. For several hours the main queue outside just got longer and longer, while the sandwich lineup sometimes rivalled it. There is a visual record in a book published thirty years later, *Pier 21* by Trudy Mitic and J.P. LeBlanc. The middle photo on page 149 shows the canteen, according to the caption "around 1950." Actually, the year was 1955, and that broad-shouldered chap, in the pale yellow sweater I can still remember, packing groceries with his back to the camera — it's me! I never worked so steadily in the rest of my life as on those boat days in the immigration canteen. If I started checking people through at four o'clock, the next time I looked at my watch it was already 7 p.m., yet it seemed that only a little while had passed. Five minutes later, I looked again and it was 9:15.

By this time, perhaps, the crowd was beginning to slacken — or perhaps not, depending on the whims of CN in getting a train ready on the tracks outside. When we were able to relax a little bit, we often found that the immigrants in the big waiting room had become positively jolly. A party atmosphere prevailed. Having endured the boredom of a week's crossing from the home port in northern or southern Europe, they had now successfully run the gauntlet of Canada's immigration inspectors, would be whisked to Montreal tomorrow, and after that Toronto, Winnipeg or who knows where — reunions with relatives, implementation of plans long postponed, realizations now imminent. For us everything was workaday, chore driven; for these newcomers to Canada, things had finally started to unfold, and this was actually the first day of the rest of their lives.

The children took it most in stride. The very youngest had drifted off to sleep; the others could not possibly do that and continued with their paper airplanes, bouncing balls and peekaboo until parents threatened violence or, worse, CN said they would be left behind. On a few occasions, in the lull before boarding the train, musicians in the crowd unsheathed their instruments; dull North American ears were treated to an interrupted international concert that went on all winter, and might be Polish, Italian, Dutch or Greek on successive boat days, depending on what ship had arrived.

As the crowd in the annex thinned out, and the train outside hooted preparations for leaving, we surveyed the canteen's emptied and thoroughly lived-in look. Invariably, the boss decided that most of the cleanup could wait until tomorrow. If it was after scheduled public transit times, he had a budget for getting employees home by taxi.

My year and a bit at Immigration made me more sophisticated and an almost-adult. I began to learn more complicated niceties of dealing with persons of varied status, from cafeteria casual to uniformed inspector. Workday stratification was weakened when we all played together at the start of the weekend. On Friday nights, the Immigration bowling league took over the basement alleys in the temporary building — previously military, but post-war, it housed the Unemployment Insurance Commission — at the corner of Hollis and Terminal Road.

The other members of our bowling foursome were an inspector, one of the guards, and a curvacious young woman my own age, who typed correspondence for the officer-in-charge. She lived in the North End. I must say, I admired her north end, south end too, and views from every other angle. Emboldened by our bowling chumdom, I asked her out a couple of times. Once I even went, unannounced and uninvited, to the door of the house where she lived with her parents. None of these approaches worked. Why was that? Toward the end of the winter, I attended a dance sponsored by the Catholic Youth Organization, and there she was on the stage, taking part in a talent contest. She sang an Irish song with a clear, true voice. I realized she was Catholic, whereas I was not only a Protestant, but a religious one at that. I was able to console myself with this explanation for the failure of my courtship gambits — and indeed, in the Halifax of that day, there were many who thought the chasm between Protestant and Catholic was both bottomless and unbridgeable.

On the longest boat days, ending after midnight, the last ones to leave the now-deserted annex were the two bosses, a pleasant woman who was our most regular casual, and me. I sat in the taxi's back seat as we wended, unless it was a weekend night, through quiet streets. All the overtime worked on a boat day would earn me an equal amount of compensating time off later in the month.

My year at Immigration was a transition — for the first time in my life, I belonged to a group of adults engaged in a common enterprise. They all thought I was grown up — so, I was.

The subtitle of the book by Mitic and LeBlanc is *The Gateway That Changed Canada*. Pier 21 changed me too. I started this work when I was only seventeen. Previously, I knew boyhood in a sheltered suburb; almost all my interests were confined within a square mile or so. Now, boy no longer, I had moved right into the mainstream of the postwar Europe-North America connection. Although my role at Immigration was a very humble one, it was part of a great Canadian enterprise with generations of tradition behind it. The crowds pulsing through Pier 21 expressed the global meaning of Halifax, which my modest efforts now helped to define.

CHAPTER 20 1957

Student Minister

Like many of my fellow students, summer was the time when you could have experiences that, for the first time, took you far away from home and familiar territory. My most formative summer experience came when I was twenty. It took me far from home and family for the first prolonged period. Alone and unsupervised, I was completely in charge of every detail of my personal life and daily routine. I had entered Dalhousie University as a theologue, accepted by the United Church as a candidate for the ministry. After my first student summer of naval training, however, I thought I had better try my hand at an active ministry. I received permission to defer my second naval summer, and I let the people at Pine Hill Divinity Hall know I was available for a summer mission field. The reply I got, mid-March, sent me scrambling for an atlas, to discover western Canada. They were appointing me the summertime student minister at Val Marie, Saskatchewan. I looked up this Val Marie: southwest corner of that foreign province — dustbowl, someone said — only a few miles north of the Montana border. Montana! And the furthest west I had previously been was Moncton.

See us then in late April, leaving Halifax in a convoy of two automobiles, both Henry Js (1953 model, Kaiser Motor Corp.) We were a total of four Dalhousie students: three student ministers and one fellow heading for summer employment at the Saskatchewan Hospital in Weyburn. After dropping off my passenger there, I proceeded, alone, along several hours of gravel road across southern Saskatchewan, as far as Cadillac. There I touched base with a lay preacher who was to be my closest colleague, although a half-hour's drive from my own location.

Val Marie was a largely Roman Catholic village, with some French still spoken. For living quarters, I was given the three-room teacherage located in the schoolyard of the Protestant school. It had an outdoor toilet, an electric range whose oven door could be left open when a bit of heat was needed in the place and a clean, concrete, undeveloped basement where I cooled the big bowls of jello I learned to make, and fixed flat tires (on my old car that had tubes that frequently needed patching) when it was raining outside.

My professional responsibilities, May to August, were to tend to a congregation at Val Marie of about one hundred (usually twenty to twenty-five attended church), and a smaller cluster of United Church people at Orkney to the south. At Val Marie, Sunday morning services were held in a small United church. The Orkney congregation (fifteen to twenty at a service) used a very pretty, very small Anglican church on Sunday evenings. There were reliable volunteer musicians to play the organ (Orkney) or piano (Val Marie) — but imagine my shock, and theirs, to discover that the most qualified person to lead singing of the familiar hymns was unmusical me.

Besides conducting services, I organized and led youth groups in both communities, held a week-long Bible school at which enthusiastic parents did almost all of the work, and visited pretty widely all of the United Church and unattached Protestant homes in the vicinity. It was in the course of these visits that I encountered a gentleman who taught me one of the most important lessons I ever learned. He was somewhat elderly, lived alone, never attended church and was held by some to be a reprobate of doubtful respectability. I enjoyed my visit with him. He said no, he would not be coming to church. He asked me if I believed in God. I said yes, of course.

He said it seemed to him that God was the sum total of people's ignorance. He laid out his thinking for me. This was the first time, I think, either in reading or in person, that I had met an advocate of atheism. In accordance with my ministerial responsibilities, I did not agree with him at the time. However, I inwardly thought there was powerful good sense in what he said. Though I resisted it, over the next several months, the idea that my reprobate Val Mariean might well be right grew. The beliefs I had set out with did not withstand his arguments, and my path as a theologue came to an end. I eventually concluded there is no God, no gods or devils — that life is just a matter of natural processes and blind chance.

CHAPTER 21 1955—58

Dalhousie

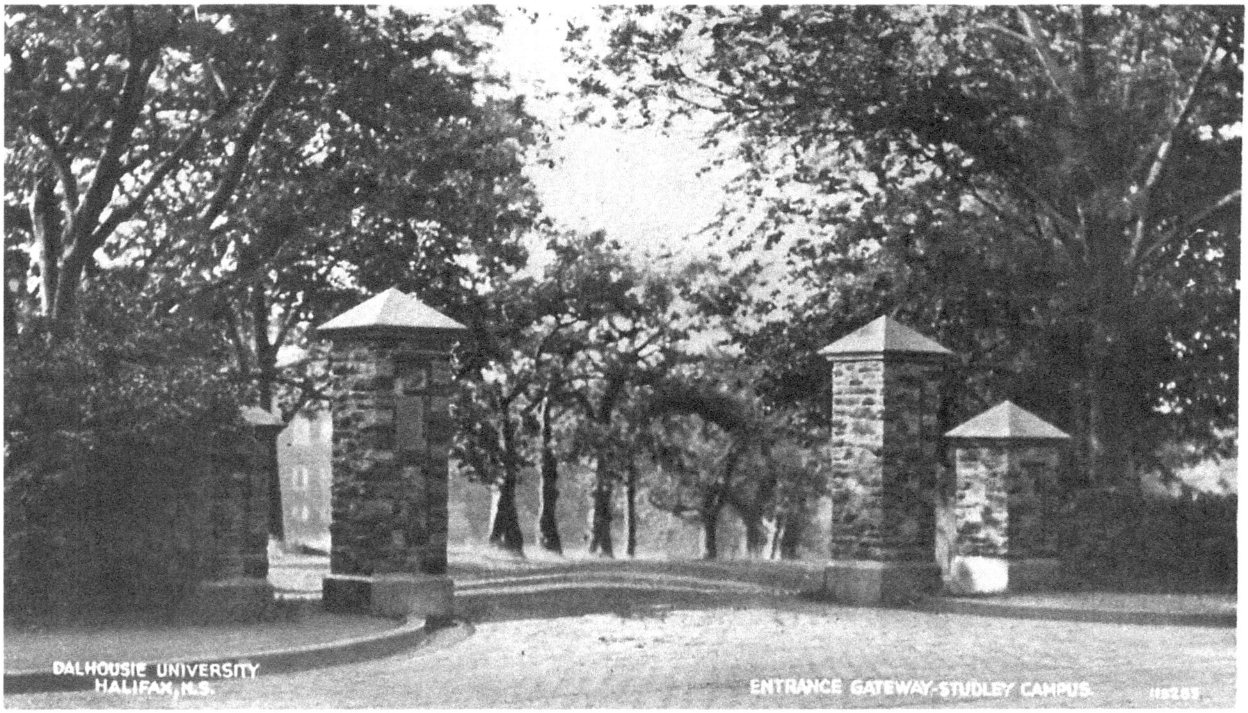

Gateway leading to Dalhousie campus from Coburg Road

Dalhousie University in the mid-1950s was a somewhat small institution of manageable proportions. Growing from 1,550 students to 1,700 during the time I was there, it was not quite cosy, but neither was it intimidating. The era of higher education for the masses had not quite arrived, and most of the students when I went there were preparing for professional careers in social work, teaching, religious leadership, law, medicine, dentistry or engineering. Since we were learning to be leaders, it is strange that the professors who guided our studies did not provide more

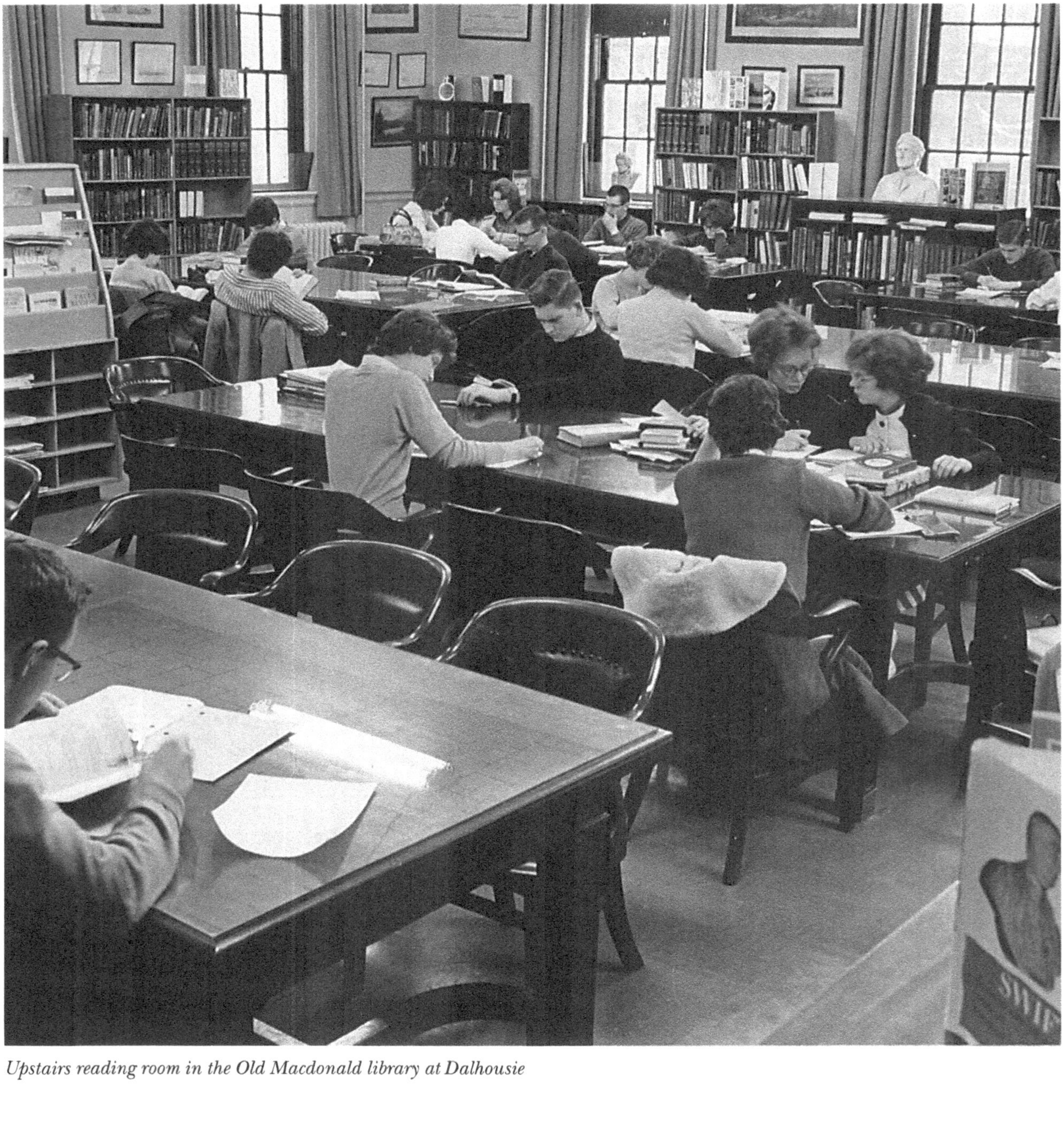

Upstairs reading room in the Old Macdonald library at Dalhousie

opportunity for us to do just that: to lead. For example, in my whole three years at Dalhousie, I do not recall even one occasion when I was called upon to make an oral presentation to the class.

Scholastically, my time at Dalhousie was successful, and for someone who was to spend most of his life in college corridors and classrooms, this introduction to the patterns and values of academic life was obviously very important. Looking back on those years, however, it seems now that no other key episode of my life was so uninteresting, even almost dull.

The dullness accusation does not apply to my student summers. They were personality-stretching and experience-deepening in many ways — new challenges, new skills and ideas, new scenes and companions. But winters at the Halifax campus were almost boring. I lived at home. Each morning, at various times dictated by my class schedule, I woke in the same small room I had occupied since I was ten. I walked down to the rotary, caught the Number 5 trolley coach going to Quinpool Road, transferred at Oxford to the belt line (numbers 2 and 3, different directions) and got off on Coburg Road. Around suppertime, I made the same trip in reverse.

There was an exception to this sameness. On Friday afternoons of my first Dalhousie year, the timetable called for a 2 p.m. to 5 p.m. laboratory class in Biology 1. Students would get a chance to handle odd parts of various creatures that Dr. Pelluet — who was, as a woman in the sciences, more of an oddity at the time than she would be now — had been discussing with us in the morning lectures. On those days, after eating my sandwich on the main (Studley) campus, I would stroll, sometimes with my friend Leroy, sometime alone, along University Avenue to the already-ancient Forrest Building.

One thing that helped make Dalhousie dull was the rigid predictability of the daily schedule. Also, our professors recognized a very narrow range of instructional or learning opportunities. Attending lectures and writing papers in some classes was contrasted with writing papers and attending lectures in others. Debates and discussions, student presentations, films and guest lecturers were almost unknown.

For me, research papers were the most exciting part of the academic routine. I loved the quiet upstairs stacks of the old Macdonald library where resources were gathered. At home, I dodged around piles of books, enjoyed immersing myself in the details of each new subject and lived for deadlines — often skipping classes the last day or two to make sure I got my best effort passed in on time.

Although living at home during my years at Dalhousie was dull, in the long-range view, I was very lucky that we lived in the city. Otherwise, getting started in university studies would have been much more challenging financially, so I do not regret it. Even though I was pretty free to come and go as I wished, daily domestic exposure to parental supervision necessarily impedes experimentation with new experiences and delays the onset of maturity.

The chief elements in a university education, no doubt, were the teachers who sat on the other end of the log. My professors at Dalhousie had many outstanding strengths. In history there was a marvellous group of role models, all different in their type of charm and academic approach. Guy MacLean turned up from somewhere or other with fact-filled lectures delivered, perhaps too fast, with indications of nervousness and solid mastery of the subject. George Wilson, nearing retirement, seemed a fountain of wisdom. At the start of a class, students would be noisily chattering. Wilson

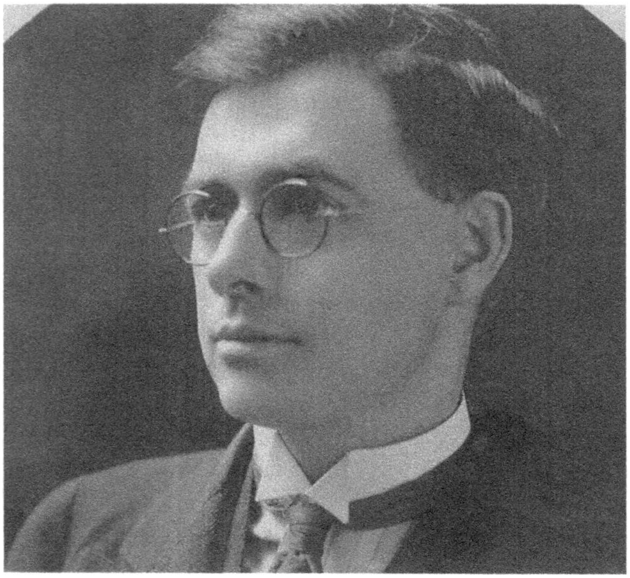

Professor C. L. Bennet

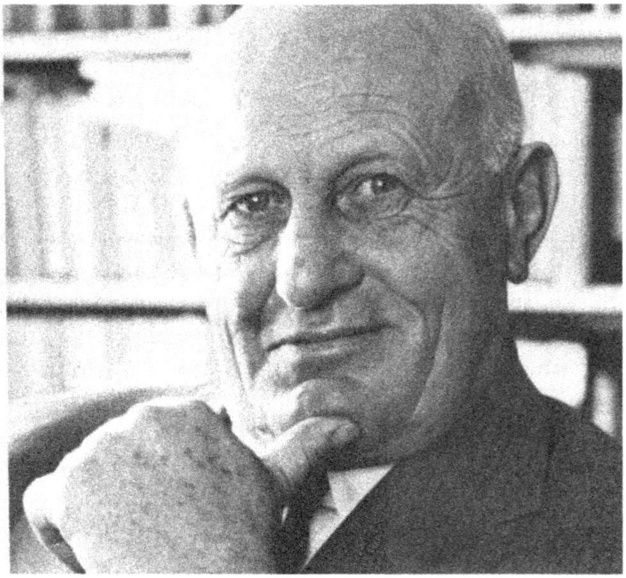

Professor George Wilson

would perch on the edge of his desk and, by beginning to discuss something in a very low voice, would command silence within a few seconds. He taught us, without saying so, that context is everything. In his .course on the French Revolution, it was about February or early March when we finally got to the events of 1789 (the year in which the Revolution is said to have begun).

Peter Waite, young and charismatic like MacLean, was as relaxed and reflective as Wilson, his mentor. Although his important published works on Canadian history had not yet begun to appear, I started edging into the subject by taking his courses on the history of the United States. I thought he demonstrated very sound judgment when, in marginal comments on the writing style in a paper I submitted, he used the words "verve" and "vivacity." I never, before or since, received such high praise for my writing.

In English, my minor subject, there were C.L. Bennet with monster Shakespeare-Milton classes, Burns-Martin of sound judgment in Canadian literature (except that he dismissed Robert Service as a mere "rhymster") and Allan Bevan. Bevan's class met in the late afternoon when energy was low; he would read suitably soulful poetry to us:

Aye lad, I lie easy . . .or
I should have been a pair of ragged claws . . .

If asked who was the best professor I had at Dalhousie, I answer all, or any, of the above. Who was the worst? There is only one candidate. I know that George Grant, head of philosophy when I was at Dalhousie, is one of the most discussed and most admired professors of his generation. I agree that he was interesting as a genuine eccentric, was quite productive, and that one of his books, *Lament for a*

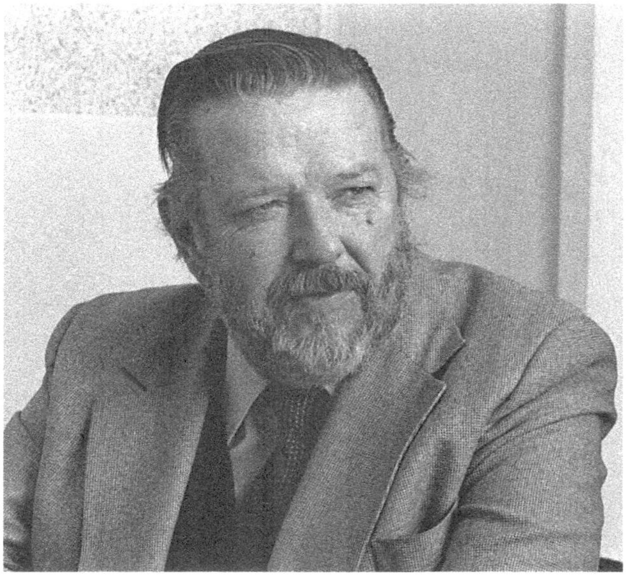

Professor George Grant

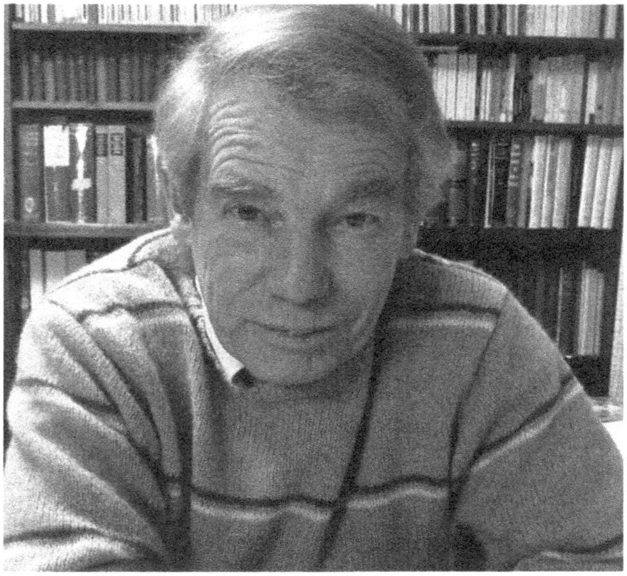

Professor Peter Waite

Nation, well deserves its status as a classic statement of the 1960s. Nevertheless, he had serious defects as a teacher.

Grant seemed to be an academic snob and elitist, permitting a small group of favoured students to carry on a cult of personality. They formed, in operatic terms, a claque that constantly sang his praises, repeated his dicta and often drew their chairs into a circle around his office desk. Others who approached could feel the barbed solidity of the psychic wall excluding those who were not part of the in group. In my first year, I took George Grant's Philosophy 1. One assignment was to choose an item from a long list, and do a review of it. I chose Dostoyevsky's novel *The Brothers Karamazov*. When I went to the library, I found that one publisher had printed it as two separate books, Part 1 and Part 2. I stared at the thickness of the two volumes, calculating how much reading time would be required before I could start writing something, and came up with a question. My question was: Do I need to review the whole work, or would it be sufficient to review either Part 1 or Part 2? At the back of my mind, I think there was also the thought that making this approach could start a warm, valuable interaction with the god-like professor.

Fifty years of reflection have taught me this may well have been a stupid question. Anyway, after screwing up my courage for about a week, I finally found Grant alone in his office and knocked on the door. He bade me enter, but did not ask me to sit down. I explained who I was and stammered out my question. He started to laugh. I was standing in front of his desk. He continued laughing. After twenty or thirty seconds, realizing that was all the answer I was going to get, I turned and slunk away.

CHAPTER 22 1956–58

The Navy

During the same week I started undergraduate classes at Dalhousie, I also joined the navy. There were posters up on campus inviting young men to apply for officer cadet status in the University Naval Training Divisions (UNTD) program. Ottawa's idea, in a scheme that had been adopted a few years earlier, was to create among the civilian population a large pool of trained, indoctrinated officers. They would be a cadre of leaders who could be called into active service if the navy needed emergency rapid expansion, as had happened during World War II.

Despite the Cold War, however, no such emergency occurred. The UNTD program can therefore be said to have missed its mark. Nevertheless, it was a powerful force helping to enrich and shape the lives of several thousand fellows like myself. It gave us a wealth of unusual, interesting experiences; an introduction to a pan-Canada, national perspective; and lucrative employment during student summers. In my case, UNTD paid most of the bills for a B.A. at Dalhousie and an M.A. at University of Toronto, while I was moved up the promotion ladder from cadet to sub-lieutenant, then lieutenant, and for three summers taught the upcoming generation of UNTDs in the navigation school (my specialty: tides) at HMCS *Stadacona* and HMCS *Cornwallis.*

Our once-weekly training sessions laid the greatest stress on two aspects of naval life: parade square drill and inspection of uniforms, to see if they were completely lint-free, with sharp creases, boots and buttons polished, sewn-on badges properly positioned and so on.

For full-time summer training, first-year cadets from all across Canada were accommodated in

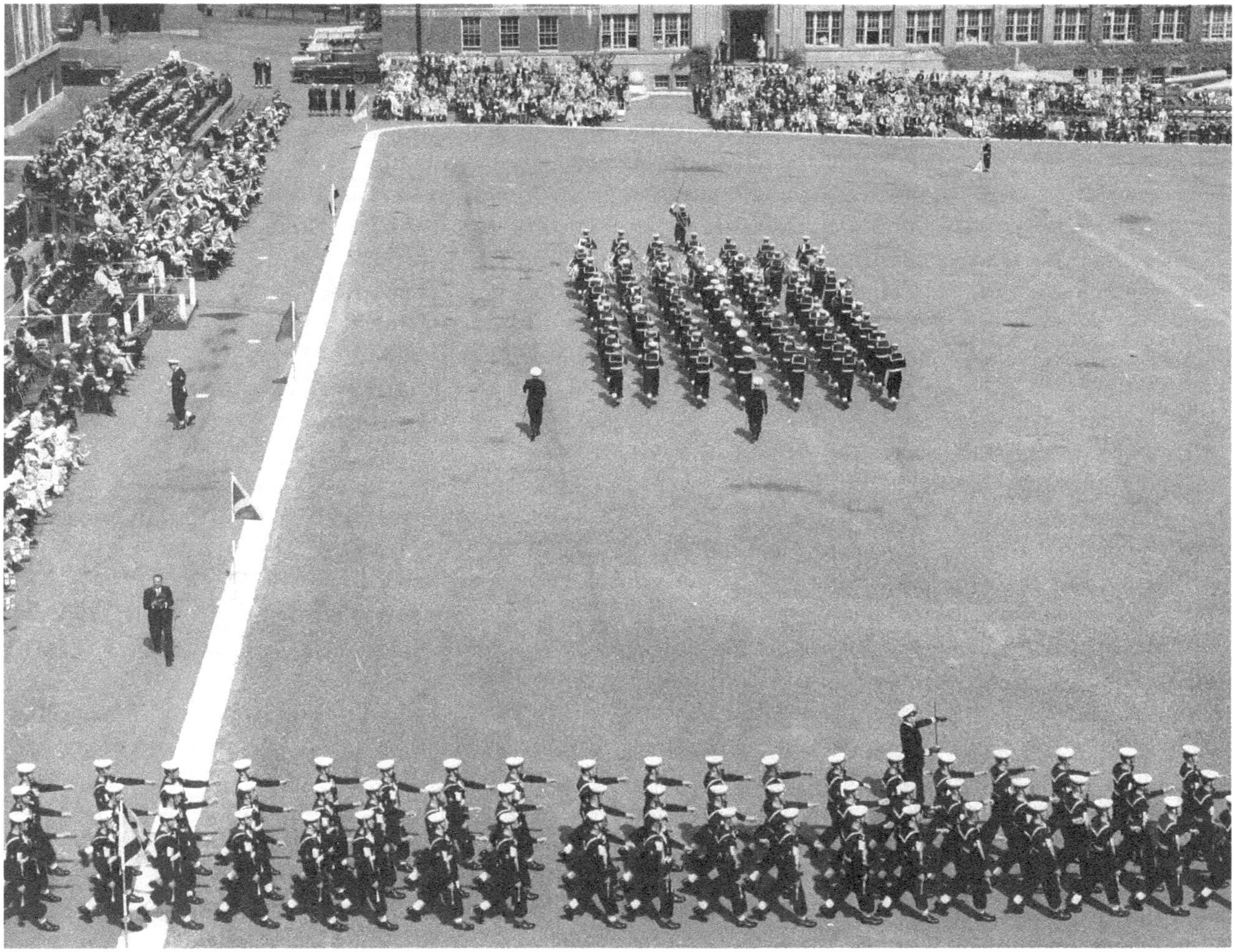

RCN band performing on the Stadacona *parade square*

barracks at the southeast corner of the huge naval base in the heart of Halifax, HMCS *Stadacona* (STAD). Some cadets travelled hundreds, even thousands of miles, to get there. In my case, I merely transferred to a different trolley coach than the one I used regularly for getting to university. Being stationed close to home meant that, like other members of the Halifax contingent, I missed elements of change and excitement that the great majority of cadets experienced. There were important compensations. Over a weekend, we could easily escape STAD's regime of petty rules and constant surveillance by visiting home. I remember a couple of times bringing new cadet friends with me. Being included in an ordinary family for a few hours helped alleviate their homesickness, and they certainly seemed to enjoy themselves, wolfing down Mother's apple pie while, wolves still, they eyed my feisty, friendly teenage sisters.

Stadacona turned out to be a complicated college for all types of naval knowledge and technology. Numerous squads of naval ratings, permanent-force officers — and we ourselves — were continually marching all over the base in small groups, to attend classes in the two- and three-week short courses, which were an Royal Canadian Navy specialty. Our studies that first summer concentrated on seamanship; recreation; communications, including Morse code and semaphore signals; torpedo and anti-submarine warfare (TAS); and the ABCs of modern navy operations rolled into a single course called ABCD (atomic/bacteriological/chemical warfare and damage control).

Three frigates from the East Coast fleet were designated to give us seagoing and shipboard experience. Towards the end of July, my group went onboard HMCS *Lauzon*. We stood regular watches (lookouts, wheelhouse) while carrying on with some of our studies and endlessly cleaning ship. The cruise took us to Plymouth and Milford Haven, Great Britain; Arcachon near Bordeaux, France (for a week, everyone had overnight leave); and Ponta Delgada, Azores. I was impressed with the immensity of the ocean, and how puny are the works of humans. Soon after getting back to Halifax, we scattered to our usual colleges.

The second summer of naval training was very similar to the first. The location changed to HMCS Naden near Victoria, B.C., and the main focus of our studies was the most difficult subject of all, celestial navigation. We spent some time in frigates (ours was HMCS *New Waterford*), but cruised only as far as Seattle.

Toward the end of August, I wanted to attend my older sister's wedding, and the considerate navy agreed to rush me home by air. It was my first flight. As the new airport at Kelly Lake was still under construction, we landed at HMCS *Shearwater*.

I was at a significant crossroads in life's dramatic journey. I had graduated with a BA from Dalhousie in the spring. Having recently abandoned the plan to become a United Church minister, the future was wide open. I thought about becoming an immigration inspector. More attractive was the idea of taking an officer's commission in the permanent force RCN. I was also attracted to the status and values of an academic career — a university professorship or high school teaching. Of the two most prestigious specialties, medicine and law, I considered my kind of bookish intelligence more suited to legal studies. So I made my decision. Unless something turned up in the next couple of weeks, after Labour Day I would register in Dalhousie Law School.

Postscript

Rereading these memoirs, my strongest impression is how very fortunate I was in the circumstances of early life. I was born into a stable, supportive family, full of love and understanding. The Armdale community was well outfitted with institutions devoted to schooling, religion and other amenities, except for public transit (and a ten-minute walk to get to the nearest stop for the Number 5 tram car was hardly a hardship). True, during my first years of school, it was a world at war. War hardly affected us, however, except for rationing, and when a close family member was killed in action, the news was kept from the children for a long time. Even after allowing for the rose-coloured-glasses syndrome which can be depended upon to improve one's memory of the past, I still seem to have been very lucky.

My initial plan for these memoirs was to make them into a book about my favourite subject, namely, me. I am not sure that has been the result. While "I" occurs frequently enough in the text, the attention of that I is often directed to the times, and the places, that provided home for my childhood. Thus, many parts of what I have written put on record features of old Halifax of fifty-five to seventy years ago: the derelict state of Melville Island prison before the Yacht Squadron moved in; the intersection of five streets at the head of the Northwest Arm before, during and after construction of the Armdale Rotary; short-lived Armdale High School at the town end of Purcell's Cove Road; children's movie club at the Oxford Theatre; skating shacks on the shore of Chocolate Lake; Jesuits patrolling their grounds on Quinpool Road before St.

Mary's College moved to the south end of Robie Street; the unchanging Dingle; and how rattling trams moved along city streets.

Other parts of my story are not so much about Halifax, or me, as about the times through which I lived. Thus we have a child's view memory of the Second World War and accounts of common experience in the 1940s and 1950s — the state of blackwhite race relations, how radio immersed us fully in North American popular culture, the games we played, prolonged courtship without sex and the worry-free acceptance of hitchhiking as a perfectly safe way to get around.

Of course, the book's discussion of all these affairs rests on my experience of them, so perhaps it is mostly about me after all. Many of my adventures and episodes were no doubt similar to, or identical with, those of other children in that time and place: learning to read, learning to swim, accent on sports, long days in school, eventually graduating to part- and full-time employments. There are three respects, however, in which my early experiences were perhaps quite different from the majority of my peers.

Attendance at Older Boys' Parliament was restricted to a small, elite group of Protestant teenagers, and helped steer me for several years into a strongly religious mode of life and ambition. Hitchhikers too were a small group, not so elite, which I enthusiastically joined from age fifteen on. I recorded all my journeys in some detail, as a historian might: Perhaps this was a hint about the future. And — here is pure luck again — I had the privilege for a year and a bit of helping land and welcome immigrants through fabled Pier 21, the gateway that changed Canada, and changed me too.

Reviewing my career options in August 1958, I decided that unless something turned up soon, I would begin studies at Dalhousie Law School that fall. This perhaps makes some readers think that the next volume of these memoirs, if any, might be titled "Life of a Lawyer." It would be a mistake to think so, because something did turn up.

In the first week of that long-ago September, I jumped at the chance to join the full-time teaching staff at The Halifax Grammar School, which was just getting organized for its first year of operation. By the end of that winter, I had decided against law school, in favour of graduate studies in history. I applied for admission to the M.A. program at University of Toronto, hopeful that a suitable title for my eventual adult memoir might be "Path of a Professor."

Acknowledgements

Somebody said, I can remember everything that ever happened, and a lot of other things besides. In composing these memoirs, I hope I have not followed the lead given by the overly optimistic second part of this formula. It is tempting, when memory flags, to fill in the blank spots with reasonable inventions. This temptation must be resisted. I have tried to stick to what I really think I recall from those distant times during and after World War II. As a result, in many places where I would have preferred to say "did" or "was" with certitude, I have had to write "seem," "perhaps" or "probably" in the interests of honesty.

This book is an account of those war and post-war times, and a travelogue of scenes and sights of old Halifax that have now disappeared. Commentary on the sights and times is interspersed with the observations and experiences of one particular young guy who noticed and understood more, one hopes, as time passed.

I owe thanks to several persons in the here and now who helped by discussing the circumstances of long ago: thanks to Heather, resident editor when she has the time and wife for life; my three sisters, Marlene, Joan and Mora; cousin Ken Cameron; Neil Fisher for his artistically-expressed interest and illustrations; Bob Gogan, the best teacher of my public school days; Dianne Landry of Dalhousie University Archives; George Kapatanakis, manager of the Armview Restaurant and Lounge; Aaron Gavel of Bell Aliant in Truro; and Gordon MacIntyre, whose boyhood in Spryfield overlapped with mine next door in Armdale.

As well, I owe recognition, and usually thanks, to a whole host of people from the past — many still with us, but many departed — who contributed to the episodes of life and learning that are put on record in these pages. Above all, Sadie and Ian, my parents; and also Albert and Johnny; Henry Aldrich and other characters who inhabited the reality of radio; Alex, the bombardier; Aunt Anabel and Uncle Archie; Miss Barton; the Bedley family, who operated a very interesting store; C.L. Bennet, Peter Waite, the Professors Usmiani and other faculty members at Dalhousie University when I studied there; Bill, Kay and the other students in Grade 12 at Armdale High School; my best friends at that stage of life, David and the other Malcolm; Lorne White; Grandma and Grandpa Cameron; Paul Campbell; Don from the trip to Boston and many other occasions; the other Don, along with George, Harold and other colleagues in elementary Greek class; the elevator man at Simpson's; hitch-hiking buddies; Hitler, Mussolini and Tojo; the Ihasz brothers; Raymond Jefferson; harassed Leo at the Oxford Theatre; Luke 2:52; Aunt Greta; Grandma MacLeod; Uncle Mel; Uncle Norman; Mr. and Mrs. Schmeisser; the canteen and kitchen staff, and other friends from my time at Pier 21; Lieutenant Trubetskoy of HMC Ships *Stadacona* and *Lauzon*; and the whole population of Val Marie, Saskatchewan, who were so kind to me in the summer of 1957.

Photo Credits

Canadian Museum of Immigration: p. 74 ('A Day In May' #6); p. 78 ('A Day In May' #21); p. 79 ('A Day In May' #23)
The Chronicle Herald: p. 6, 7, 8, 9, 10, 11 (bottom), 12, 13, 14,
Dalhousie University Archives: p. 83 (PCI 43-3-1); p. 86 (both); p. 87 (both)
Fort Sackville Historical Society: p. 59 (#589-1)
Halifax Library: p. 19 (#95 211); p. 27 (#WM 93 7 2); p. 69 (WM HPL-PC-F0038)
Jeffries, Charlotte: p. 49
Longard, Alfred Heartz: p. 11 (top)
MacLeod, Malcolm: p. 25, 35, 50, 61, 63, 64 (both)
Nova Scotia Archives: p. 15 (Bollinger #105); p. 16 (Bollinger #4924-2); p. 18 (Bollinger # 4739-1); p. 24 (Norwood #409); p. 26 (200802318); p. 30 (Bollinger #270B); p. 31 (Bollinger #270A); p. 32 (Bollinger #618-A); p. 54 (Bollinger #4830-3); p. 66 (Norwood #503-39); p. 71 (Bollinger #4931); p. 75 (Norwood #61); p. 89 (12635)

Index